ORDINARY GRACE
WEEKS 1–17

ORDINARY GRACE
WEEKS 1–17

Daily Gospel Reflections

By the Daughters of St. Paul

Edited by Maria Grace Dateno, FSP
and Marianne Lorraine Trouvé, FSP

Pauline
BOOKS & MEDIA
Boston

Library of Congress Cataloging-in-Publication Data

Ordinary grace weeks 1-17 : daily Gospel reflections / by the Daughters of St. Paul ; edited by Maria Grace Dateno and Marianne Lorraine Trouvé.

   p. cm.

 ISBN 0-8198-5442-5 (pbk.)

 1. Bible. N.T. Gospels--Meditations. 2. Church year meditations. 3. Catholic Church--Prayers and devotions. 4. Catholic Church. Lectionary for Mass (U.S.). 5. Common lectionary (1992) I. Dateno, Maria Grace. II. Trouvé, Marianne Lorraine. III. Daughters of St. Paul.

 BS2555.54.O73 2011

 242'.3--dc22

2010026125

Cover design by Rosana Usselmann

Cover photo Mary Emmanuel Alves, FSP

"P" and PAULINE are registered trademarks of the Daughters of St. Paul.

Published by Pauline Books & Media, 50 Saint Pauls Avenue, Boston, MA 02130-3491

Printed in the U.S.A.

www.pauline.org

Pauline Books & Media is the publishing house of the Daughters of St. Paul, an international congregation of women religious serving the Church with the communications media.

1 2 3 4 5 6 7 8 9   13 12 11 10

Contents

How to Use This Book

∴∙∙∙∙∙∙∙∙∙∙∙∴

*"Grace to you and peace from God our Father
and the Lord Jesus Christ" (Rom 1:7).*

Every day, God's grace is available through his word. There is, of course, nothing "ordinary" about grace, which is the amazing reality of God's life in us. There is nothing "ordinary" about Ordinary Time, either. In fact, the term "Ordinary Time" does not mean time that is average or mundane. It comes from the way the weeks are "ordered" using numbers in the form of ordinals (first, second, third, etc.).

Ordinary Time is a time of grace, an opportunity to reflect on all the aspects of the mystery of Christ, rather than intensely focusing on a certain aspect, as we do in the other liturgical seasons. You are invited to share with the Daughters of St. Paul their meditations on the Gospel readings of Ordinary Time.

These pages are based on *Lectio Divina* (holy reading), which is a way of praying with Scripture. Our founder, Blessed James Alberione, urged us to nourish ourselves with the Scriptures. He said that when we do this, we "experience interiorly the kindling of a divine fire." Many methods of *Lectio Divina* have developed since the time of early monasticism. Here, the sisters use a simple framework that allows the word of God to make room in our minds and hearts.

The first step, *Lectio* (reading), is to read the day's Gospel passage from a missal or Bible. Read it a few times slowly, perhaps especially noticing the phrase or verse that is listed under the *Meditatio* section.

Next, the *Meditatio* (meditation) expands the meaning of this phrase and explores what it is saying to us today—what God is asking of us, or challenging us to, or offering to us. After reading the meditation, take as much time as you wish to reflect on it.

The *Oratio* (prayer) can help you talk to God about what has arisen in your heart, so that the time of prayer becomes a conversation, not just a time to think. God has spoken in the Scripture. We hear the invitation in our meditation, but now a response is called for. Our response is not just to say, "Yes, I want to do as you are asking me," but also to say, "Help me do it, Lord!"

The short line under *Contemplatio* (contemplation) is a way of extending this time of prayer into life. You can silently repeat it throughout the day to help deepen the intimacy with the Lord that you experienced in prayer.

Thanks be to God!

Liturgical Calendars

⟨·············⟩

Note to the reader: Each liturgical year the Church celebrates thirty-four weeks of Ordinary Time in two sections. The seasons of Advent, Christmas, Lent, and Easter take up the other weeks of the year. The liturgical year begins with the first Sunday of Advent.

The First Week of Ordinary Time begins on the Monday after the Feast of the Baptism of the Lord, which concludes the Christmas season. The weeks of Ordinary Time continue in order until Lent begins on Ash Wednesday.

The Easter season runs from Easter Sunday until Pentecost, and Ordinary Time resumes on the Monday after Pentecost. The numbered weeks usually then pick up from the point where they left off, but sometimes a few weeks are skipped.

The two Sundays after Pentecost, Trinity Sunday and Corpus Christi, replace the numbered Sundays of Ordinary Time that would otherwise fall on those days.

The chart on page 4 indicates the dates for the beginning of each section of Ordinary Time:

YEAR	ORDINARY TIME BEGINS AFTER THE BAPTISM OF THE LORD	ORDINARY TIME RESUMES AFTER PENTECOST
2011	January 10 (Monday of First Week)	June 13 (Eleventh week)
2012	January 10 (Tuesday of First Week)	May 28 (Eighth week)
2013	January 14 (Monday of First Week)	May 20 (Seventh week)
2014	January 13 (Monday of First Week)	June 9 (Tenth week)
2015	January 12 (Monday of First Week)	May 25 (Eighth week)
2016	January 11 (Monday of First Week)	May 16 (Seventh week)
2017	January 10 (Tuesday of First Week)	June 5 (Ninth week)
2018	January 9 (Tuesday of First Week)	May 21 (Seventh week)
2019	January 14 (Monday of First Week)	June 10 (Tenth week)
2020	January 13 (Monday of First Week)	June 1 (Ninth week)
2021	January 11 (Monday of First Week)	May 24 (Eighth week)
2022	January 10 (Monday of First Week)	June 6 (Tenth week)

The Sunday readings follow a three-year cycle (A, B, or C) as indicated in the following chart:

Year	Cycle
2011	Cycle A
2012	Cycle B
2013	Cycle C
2014	Cycle A
2015	Cycle B
2016	Cycle C
2017	Cycle A
2018	Cycle B
2019	Cycle C
2020	Cycle A
2021	Cycle B
2022	Cycle C

Monday of the First Week
of Ordinary Time

∴ · · · · · · · · · · · · ∴

Lectio

Mark 1:14–20

Meditatio

"This is the time of fulfillment. The kingdom of God is at hand."

Now is the time. Mark uses the Greek word *kairos*, which means the appointed time or the favored time. The reading for today, the first day of Ordinary Time, reminds me of a professor who walks into the first class of the year and immediately launches into an overview of the course. The first twenty minutes of the lecture telegraph that this semester will move along at a good clip. Looking for a blow-off course? Here's your cue to look elsewhere. Resolve to keep up with the readings and assignments, and you'll learn something worthwhile.

Today's Gospel has a sense of urgency. Today, in this moment, the kingdom of God draws near. God's Good News—the Gospel—demands a response, and it will not leave us uneffected. God's call is magnetic. Simon, Andrew, James, and John drop everything to follow Jesus. Matthew's parallel account of this scene (4:18–22) gives us a sense that more was involved in the call of the first disciples, but Mark stresses that the kingdom of God is at hand *now*. Do something about it *now*.

The endless stream of ordinary "now" moments is the setting for the kingdom of God in our real world. This present moment is the place of God's gift to us, and our gift to God. Neither the past with its mistakes or triumphs, nor the future with all its variables, concerns us now. We can play the game of *should-have-been* and *could-have-done*, but it doesn't change reality. We can imagine ourselves in wonderfully ideal circumstances or cringe at foreseeable calamities, but the future is never as rosy or bleak in the way that we've imagined it. All we have is today. God calls us today. Jesus passes by this morning, and he proclaims the Good News: "This is the time of fulfillment. The kingdom of God is at hand."

Oratio

Lord, the spotlight of holiday festivities is over, and now it is back to the day-to-day routine. Welcome to the "ordinary time" of my life. This present moment is where we meet. You are fully here. Am I fully here too? Lord, you know how much time and energy I spend rehashing past events as well as dreaming of or dreading the future. Help me to live this moment to the full. I want to be here with you—now. May your kingdom come in the midst of my daily routine.

Contemplatio

May your kingdom come in the midst of my daily routine.

Tuesday of the First Week
of Ordinary Time

⁚············⁚

Lectio

Mark 1:21–28

Meditatio

> *"The people were astonished at his teaching. . . ."*

Interesting words: *the people were astonished.* They don't clap. They aren't taken aback. They don't have an animated discussion after his proclamation. Rather they are stunned into silence. The people are excited that they have finally found a teaching that answers the deepest questions and hungers of their heart.

We *want* to be taught. We look for a master at living. No matter how smart we may feel ourselves to be, we still are gratefully amazed when we encounter preaching that reveals a dimension of life or truth beyond the commonplace. We long to know there is something more to our lives, a deeper, ultimate meaning to the daily grind, something that makes it all worthwhile.

The astonishment of the crowds listening to Jesus is all the more intriguing when we recall that Jesus preaches values that turn the conventional wisdom of the world upside down, often uncomfortably so. The world's values don't astonish. For all their glitter, they tire and bore us, exhaust, confuse, and defeat us.

The values taught by Jesus, on the other hand, even today bring light, hope, and the welcome element of surprise. They almost always point out an unexpected path, one that is inexplicable and incomprehensible, one that reduces us to reverent tears and quiet homage when we encounter it.

Jesus teaches you and me personally. His classrooms are myriad because he understands his students well and knows just how to get a word or light through the slightest crack we sometimes leave open. We find him teaching us in homilies and movies, in the teachings of the Church and the suggestions of a neighbor, in a magazine article or in the innocent prayer of a child. The movie theater becomes a "sanctuary," and the place where we read a document becomes a chapel. We meet Jesus, personally, like the men in the synagogue or the man with the unclean spirit in today's reading.

Oratio

Jesus, speak to me a word that will bring water to my parched spirit. A word that will point out an unexpected direction for me in some difficulty I am experiencing.

Contemplatio

Master, I am waiting on your word.

Wednesday of the First Week
of Ordinary Time

❖ · · · · · · · · · · · · ❖

Lectio

Mark 1:29–39

Meditatio

> *"Rising very early before dawn, he left and went off*
> *to a deserted place, where he prayed."*

In this passage, Mark recounts a whirlwind of activity on the part of Jesus in Capernaum. Having taught in the synagogue the previous morning and expelled a demon, Jesus then subdues the fever of Peter's mother-in-law. At sunset—once the Sabbath is over—Jesus responds to the needs of the crowds swarming around the door of the house where he is staying. Before sunrise, he is on the move again—but in a different way. He is going to a lonely spot to commune with his Father before departing for other towns to teach and heal there also.

In these lines, Mark shows us Jesus' compassion, dedication, prayerfulness, and zeal. He also shows us another quality—Jesus' balance. Jesus slept and prayed before resuming his work.

It's good to consider Jesus' balance, because sometimes we can get out of kilter. Our lives can become so busy that our rest and our prayer life often suffer. As a result, our whole being suffers.

Admittedly, balance is hard to achieve in our society, especially for breadwinners. Yet without balance, life grows frustrating, and burnout becomes a real possibility. *Homo sapiens* are supposed to be wise. Each of us should be able to schedule short breaks for rest and/or prayer. Even a five-minute break can be refreshing. A fifteen-minute break is even better.

Once, while I was visiting a friend in a coastal town, she gave me a tour of the area and then pulled up to an overlook that offered a breathtaking view of the sea at sunset, with the surf breaking on the shining rocks. We stayed there for a while, silently contemplating the scene. "Every evening after work, I spend a few minutes here," she told me. "You'd be surprised how many others do the same."

Perhaps each of us can find our own "overlook," even if it's within us.

Oratio

Jesus, teach me how to *live my life*. Help me to delight in a vista; savor a meal; enjoy the company of family and friends; relax during break time; walk, jog, or run; and hold brief conversations with you as I go about my daily routine. Don't let me become (or remain) a workaholic. Your gift of life is too precious to be lived only partially.

Contemplatio

Lord, teach me to live!

Thursday of the First Week
of Ordinary Time

∴ . . . . ∴

Lectio

Mark 1:40–45

Meditatio

"He spread the report abroad . . ."

Today's Gospel starts out dramatically: a man with leprosy approaches Jesus, falls to his knees, and makes a striking act of faith: "If you wish, you can make me clean." Jesus does will it. With a word and a touch, Jesus heals the man and then gives him the impossible command: "See that you tell no one anything. . . ."

Not only was the healed man totally incapable of obeying that command, but he was also amazingly effective in proclaiming what Jesus did for him. A real networker, he "began to publicize the whole matter"; "he spread the report abroad so that . . . people kept coming to [Jesus] *from everywhere.*"

A similar thing happened in the 1950s with a Franciscan community in the Midwest. One of the elderly priests, Solanus Casy, was being transferred back to the friary in Detroit for health care. The problem was that Father Solanus was renowned in the area because of the astounding healings that came about through his prayers. If the people of Detroit learned that their beloved Father Solanus was back, the community would be mobbed. The brothers managed to keep quiet, but the superiors hadn't taken the media into account. A newspaper report of the Capuchin community's one-hundredth anniversary put Father Solanus on the front page, and the doorbell began ringing. When he died (within the year), some 10,000 people came to pay their respects to the man who taught them to "thank God ahead of time."

And still now, the whole world is waiting for a word about Jesus.

Oratio

Lord, you have not called me to be silent. Quite the contrary! "Go into the whole world and proclaim the gospel to every creature" (Mk 16:15). Yet sometimes I am hard put to find in myself the faith that the man with leprosy had, a faith that moved you so deeply. Today, help me to be extra alert to notice the subtle signs of your presence, your love, your grace. Then, with the man healed of leprosy, with Father Solanus, with your apostles after the resurrection, I would say "it is impossible for us not to speak about what we have seen and heard" (Acts 4:20).

Contemplatio

"Give thanks to the LORD who is good, whose love endures forever" (Ps 118:1).

Friday of the First Week
of Ordinary Time

∴⋯⋯⋯⋅∴

Lectio

Mark 2:1–12

Meditatio

> *"When Jesus saw their faith, he said to [the paralytic],*
> *'Child, your sins are forgiven.'"*

Today's Gospel account is one of the few occasions when Jesus cures someone because of the faith of others. Because of the faith of the people who lower the paralyzed man through the roof, Jesus forgives his sins and heals him. What a gift those faith-filled people gave to the crippled man!

The text does not indicate why the paralytic had no faith. People lose their faith for many reasons. Perhaps the paralytic *did* believe but could not communicate it. Perhaps the fact that he was paralyzed caused him to doubt.

The key may be in the way that Jesus tenderly addresses the paralytic with the term "Child." Perhaps Jesus is touching the heart of what had been ruptured in the paralytic due to his physical infirmity—his relationship with God as his father who is taking care of him.

This passage, then, speaks volumes to me. It indicates to me that God wants to relate to me as my Father as well. At times, my own faith has been paralyzed. When my heart has ached because of grief, when my faith has been shattered because I could not understand the illness of a loved one, I too have doubted that God is my Father. At those times when my faith lay helpless, someone else's faith may have been carrying me. It is comforting to know that at those times in my life, others carried me in their faith.

When we are in the presence of another whose faith is paralyzed, it is often so difficult to know what to do, what words of encouragement we can offer to strengthen another's faith. This passage, then, is a consoling one. It tells us that in those moments we can believe for others—we can carry them in our faith. And Jesus will somehow allow them to hear him speak the word, "Child," and restore them.

Oratio

Father! Thank you for revealing yourself to us as a Father. Help me to see the many ways that you are taking care of me, providing for me, watching over me with fatherly love and concern. So many ways that you do this are hidden to me, especially the ones that are so ordinary—the sun's warm touch, the wind's cool breath, the water's comforting embrace. May these tangible elements that you have created remind me again and again of your love for me as my creator—my Father. Amen.

Contemplatio

Child, you are precious in my eyes and I love you (see Is 43:4).

Saturday of the First Week
of Ordinary Time

⁝ . . . . ⁝

Lectio

Mark 2:13–17

Meditatio

> *"I did not come to call the righteous but sinners."*

This passage of Mark shows us once again how comfortable Jesus was with people from every stratum of society. Levi, the tax collector, is not regarded as fit company by the religious leaders of his times. Yet Jesus is pleased to include him in his circle of friends, even to sit at his table and dine with him. This is not only a sign of friendship or fellowship but also a gesture of real intimacy.

Certainly Levi knows his sinfulness. His own people, who avoid him, hurl bitter words at him, and look down on him, remind him of it every day. But Jesus pays no attention to these judgmental gestures. When he sees Levi sitting at his post, Jesus looks deeper than others and sees something in Levi that others do not. Then Jesus calls him to be one of his followers.

Jesus' acceptance of Levi's invitation to eat in his home must have been such a surprise, such a consolation! This is the wonder and beauty of our God, for he calls us in our "sickness," in our "sinfulness," and surprises us with his love and forgiveness.

Saint Paul reminds us that God shows his love for us because Christ died for us while we were still sinners (see Rom 5:8). So, like Levi, we all need a Savior, a divine Physician to heal us. This Physician will reveal to us our weaknesses, will speak to us words of comfort and hope, and will finally heal us so that we can be healthy bearers of his name.

The call for each of us is to accept our condition as sinners, to relax, wipe away the fear and pray: "Come, Lord, into our houses, into our lives. Heal us and enfold us in your embrace of love!"

Oratio

Lord, Eternal Physician, I would like to consider myself among the healthy and virtuous. It feels more comfortable, more prestigious. Yet that is not the kind of person you call. You call those who know they are sinners. And in all honesty, when I look within myself, I see my weak and unhealthy state. Help me, like Levi, to acknowledge my sinfulness, my weaknesses. Isn't this the first step toward change? Lord, take me by the hand and lead me one step at a time toward what you consider to be true virtue, true health!

Contemplatio

Those who are healthy do not need a physician, but the sick do.

Second Sunday of Ordinary Time —
Year A

❖ · · · · · · · · · · · · ❖

Lectio

John 1:29–34

Meditatio

> ". . . I came baptizing with water . . .
> that he might be made known to Israel."

John speaks these words the day after his limpid testimony to the representatives of the religious authorities in Jerusalem, "I am not the Messiah" (Jn 1:20).

How John's heart must be swelling with recognition as he sees the humble Jesus approaching! How the mysterious moment of Jesus' baptism must be flooding back into his consciousness, the moment when the one who sent him made John realize that this praying Jesus was the one who baptizes with the Holy Spirit. How much awe and gratitude John must feel as he sees the pieces falling into place! John's response of generous love will be forever the model for a disciple to imitate, as he testifies that Jesus "is the Son of God."

John's followers stand transfixed—is this really what they are hearing? Is John saying that there is another to whom they would turn for leadership?

To stand back and present another requires great strength of character, great humility. But John has always lived with all his soul in the realm of the truth, and for him, this is the moment he has been waiting for. John is so much a part of the advent of the Messiah that the word "detachment" is not enough to describe the greatness of John's generous response to Jesus' coming. Jesus is the bridegroom, and John is the "best man" who "rejoices greatly at the bridegroom's voice" (Jn 3:29).

May Jesus lead us, too, into that world of love and joy that humble souls inhabit, souls who, like John, know and make known to all who will listen, that "this is the Son of God."

Oratio

Jesus, help me remember that those who follow you must pass through the valley of uncertainty, with few signs to help them see their way. John is my model, who hung on to the fire within, dark though the way may have been. Teach me to be aware of the signs that are sewn into the fabric of everyday life, signs that will lead me to the moment of recognition and love, when you will fully reveal yourself to me as "the Son of God," whom I seek to follow forever.

Contemplatio

"That he might be made known. . . ."

Second Sunday of Ordinary Time—
Year B

❖ ⋯⋯⋯⋯⋯ ❖

Lectio

John 1:35–42

Meditatio

"Behold, the Lamb of God . . ."

Breathing deeply, I place myself into this scene of the Gospel. I listen and watch, knowing that it is good for me to be here. The word is alive, vibrant, and I want this life-giving word to be part of my life. So I take my life to the word and with the Teacher's help, place myself into this scene.

I see John as he stands with two of his disciples. I don't need to go and stand with them. Rather, I watch and see what is going to happen. He has just told them, "Behold, the Lamb of God." It calls for a response. It's quite a statement, quite an invitation. It calls for even more excitement and gratitude than if someone told me, "I'm going to give you two free tickets to the New York City Ballet . . . or to the Super Bowl." Yes, I would respond and be grateful! But here is John, offering something entirely more wondrous, saying, "Look, there goes the Lamb of God. Don't miss this. Look alive, pay attention."

I'm glad to see that the disciples are attentive; they leave John and follow Jesus. Not only are their eyes and ears open, but also their hearts. They speak to the Teacher, they follow him, they stay with him. We know too, through the various stories of the New Testament, that they continued to listen and to follow him, even amid confusion and misunderstanding. They continued to respond to the invitation that I am witnessing today: "Behold. . . ." They continued to be attentive and to appreciate the gift offered to them, the unimaginable gift of following Christ closely.

Ordinary Time may be "ordered" (as in numbered and organized), but it is certainly not "ordinary." I am being called to follow the Lamb of God, to throw my lot in with his, to walk in his blessed steps.

Oratio

Jesus, just being alive means I have been called into life by the Father. Your word and your invitation seek to make that life even richer by binding me to yourself. Make me attentive to life and its circumstances, so as to see you hiding there. Help me listen to the many calls you place in my path this day. I trust you to nudge me in the right direction, to give me the right words of compassion, to ask the right questions to show caring. You have blessed me. Give me the attentiveness and care I need today to be a blessing to others.

Contemplatio

Holy Lamb of God, I am so grateful for your invitations.

Second Sunday of Ordinary Time—
Year C

⋮· · · · · · · · · · · ·⋮

Lectio

John 2:1–11

Meditatio

> ". . . you have kept the good wine until now."

Jesus and his mother are attending a neighbor's wedding in Cana with many other people, including his disciples. The couple is celebrating the first day of their new shared life, blessed by the presence of family and friends. But then the unthinkable happens. The waiters, who had been generously serving wine to the guests, noticed that the supply is running low. Now the headwaiter discreetly approaches the bridegroom to inform him of the problem.

Mary, ever attentive, notices and brings the problem to her Son. He feigns unconcern. "How does your concern affect me? My hour has not yet come." But Mary knows him and tells the waiters to do whatever her Son suggests. Jesus realizes that his Mother has provided the occasion, and he decides that this is the hour he has awaited. He scans the scene and chooses the large stone jars used to hold water for ceremonial washing. He tells the waiters: "Fill the jars with water." Each jar holds twenty to thirty gallons of water, and the waiters fill them to the brim. Jesus appears satisfied with this and does nothing further. We can imagine the waiters looking at one another and shrugging their shoulders as if let down. Quietly observing their reaction, Jesus then tells them, "Draw some out now and take it to the headwaiter." They are stunned when the headwaiter approaches the bridegroom and gently chides him for saving such good wine until the end of the celebration.

This is the miracle of beginnings. Not only is it the first of Jesus' miraculous signs, but it is also the first glimpse of his glory. The disciples are beginning to sense that their new friend is a very special individual. And we, from our present perspective, can see reflected in this miracle the continual transformation of water and wine into the Lord's sacred Blood in our celebrations of the Eucharist. Are we still amazed by this miracle in our midst?

Oratio

Dear Jesus, Mary's Son, we are always amazed and most grateful for the signs you work before our eyes and within our hearts. You are attentive to our needs and ready to step in with the gift of your grace. You show us your care through your sacramental presence and through those with whom you have graced our lives. Keep us aware, so that we never miss these miracles of love. Amen.

Contemplatio

Jesus and his Mother were invited.

Monday of the Second Week
of Ordinary Time

⁝ · · · · · · · · · · · · ⁝

Lectio

Mark 2:18–22

Meditatio

"New wine . . . fresh wineskins."

The Gospel selections this week describe the newness both of the message Jesus announced and of the response that his message calls for. This is most explicit in today's reading. Jesus is not contrasting works of the Law with faith. Judaism always focused on faith in God, not on the Law for its own sake. The prophets of Israel insisted on this and on wholehearted devotion to God. Then what's so new about this "good news"?

Paul would later develop the important point Jesus makes today: Jesus himself, not the ascetic practices of religion, is the Way to this wholehearted response to God. Mercy is now the path to justice (God's restoration of the human person), a mercy incarnated in the person of Jesus, God's self-revelation. Jesus is Israel's bridegroom, a title the prophets ascribed only to God. This bold, radical claim is essential to legitimize Jesus' call to that change of heart needed for grasping and accepting his message.

Moreover, in today's passage, Jesus hints at the paschal mystery and beyond: even future ascetic practices—prayer, virtue, working for justice—will assume a new dimension when the bridegroom is taken away. Mark implies that these will reach their full evangelical potential in light of that "day" when Christ will return in glory to claim forever the bride the Father has chosen for him.

Jesus' message moves discipleship to a new plane. He is saying it's time for a paradigm shift. Sometimes we tend to enshrine as untouchable "tradition" those things that are little more than the familiar. We may then impose our tradition on others, indicating perhaps where we invest our identity or security. Instead, what would it take for us, for *me*, to accept the Spirit's action in my life? What would I have to relinquish and what would I have to take up? What would change look like? Do I *want* to pay the price for a new wineskin?

Oratio

Lord Jesus, some of the old wine I've been storing has soured. Some is good in itself, but doesn't mix well with what you want to do in me. Where are you leading me? To embrace a new approach to prayer? To forgive someone, or ask forgiveness? What new attitude do I need toward people in our world or in my personal relationships? Make of me a new garment and a new vessel, that I might honor and warm others by the way I live your word.

Contemplatio

I trust you and entrust myself to your re-creation.

Tuesday of the Second Week of Ordinary Time

∴ · · · · · · · · · · · · ∴

Lectio

Mark 2:23–28

Meditatio

"Look."

Isn't it amazing how several people can look at the same event but *see* something entirely different? The Gospel recounts a day in the life of Jesus. "Jesus was passing through a field of grain" and "his disciples began to make a path while picking the heads of grain." Mark's Gospel places this scene after a series of encounters Jesus has had with sinners and tax collectors. It seems that some of the Pharisees have grown exasperated with Jesus' "undisciplined behavior" and they let him know it.

So the Pharisees speak up *again* and confront Jesus, "Look, why are they doing what is unlawful on the Sabbath?"

Is that all they can see—that the law of the Sabbath is being broken? Is there more to the situation than immediately meets the eye?

Can they see that the disciples are accompanied by the Messiah, the Son of God? Can they see the compassion and providence of God who is Father and chooses to provide for his children's needs through the nature he created? Can they be awed by a God who actually cares for and gets involved in the lives of his creatures? These are all "revolutionary" visions, hard to believe, yet those who have eyes to see can see it.

As we go through our day, what do we point out to ourselves, to God, to others? What are we seeing when we say, "Look!"? Is our vision dominated by a narrow, self-righteous perspective at times? Do we think we've got a handle on a situation that we just walked in on? Do we ever even stop to ask ourselves: "What is happening here beyond what I catch at first sight?" Am I willing to let God show me something different from what immediately meets my eye?

Oratio

Lord, my vision can be so narrow. I tend to see what I want to see, without leaving you space to show me what *really* is. Could it be that if I let you show me something different, something deeper, something new, that I would have to change? It's easy to get used to seeing life as I have always seen it, to use experiences and events around me to confirm *my* ideas and prejudices. Forgive me, Lord, for making myself the measure of truth, of reality. Today, let me *let you* say to me, "Look!" And may I see what you see.

Contemplatio

"Master, I want to see" (Mk 10:51).

Wednesday of the Second Week
of Ordinary Time

∴· · · · · · · · · · · ·∴

Lectio

Mark 3:1–6

Meditatio

"They watched Jesus closely."

People who tried to trip Jesus up through questions or challenges were bound to fail. He brought such an unusual perspective to any verbal test, cutting straight to the heart of it, that those who posed the questions ended up as befuddled as they had hoped Jesus would be. So they couldn't trick Jesus intellectually. But they knew that the one sure way to get him was to bring him face to face with suffering. And we find several places in the Gospel where sick or crippled people are used as decoys to lure Jesus into "inappropriate" or "illegal" healing on the Sabbath.

In today's Gospel, Jesus walks into just such a trap. His adversaries, hoping to catch him in the act of violating the Sabbath, position a helpless man in Jesus' path. The man's hand is weak and probably paralyzed. Jesus would never just smile and nod at the poor man and then go pray as usual, and everyone in the synagogue knows it. We can only imagine how charged the atmosphere must be. But Jesus turns the tables on them all with a setup of his own: "Is it lawful to do good on the Sabbath?" In response to their silence, Jesus turns toward the crippled man and tells him, "Stretch out your hand."

Like David, who literally risked his life on God's faithfulness when he went against Goliath, Jesus puts his own life on the line in order to restore the health of that unfortunate in the synagogue. Mark says, "The Pharisees went out and immediately took counsel with the Herodians against him to put him to death."

Oratio

Jesus, you went to the synagogue that Sabbath to pray and ended up in a showdown, but the gauntlet thrown down was a suffering human being. Your adversaries watched your every move, but you gazed elsewhere. When you looked at that man's useless, withered hand, the words of Psalm 137 must have come to mind immediately: "If I forget you, Jerusalem, may my right hand wither!" (v. 5). What was Jerusalem if not "the Lord's footstool" (see Is 66:1), the place where God's glory dwells (see Ps 26:8)? And where does God's glory dwell more than in "the human person fully alive," as Saint Irenaeus would later say? Bringing that man back to fullness of life, you made it clear that you were doing God's work, and that it was and is the power of God, the power of a life that cannot be destroyed (see Heb 7:16), at work in you.

Contemplatio

"Your right hand saves me" (Ps 138:7).

Thursday of the Second Week
of Ordinary Time

⁚· · · · · · · · · · · ·⁚

Lectio

Mark 3:7–12

Meditatio

"He told his disciples to have a boat ready for him . . ."

I don't usually think of Jesus as needing my help. Jesus can manage a storm, or feed a multitude. Yet, in today's passage Jesus doesn't seem to have everything under control. He seems concerned that the crowd might crush him. So he tells his disciples to get a boat ready for him so he can slip away.

When Jesus says, "have a boat ready for me," what does that mean for me today? He is both asking for my help and inviting himself into my space. Jesus may invite himself into my boat in many ways and through many people. Will I have my boat ready for him?

My first reaction to this question is "No, I don't have my boat ready for you." Today's Gospel reminds me of a similar passage from Luke's Gospel, where Jesus steps into Peter's boat—empty of fish and full of messy, tangled nets.

We often invite God in when we "have things in order" and feel a sense of accomplishment. When areas of our life are out of order we tell God, "I'll get back to you tonight when I have a few quiet minutes, then we can talk." But God does not want to wait until the evening to hear about the problems of my day. God, in Jesus, literally wants to step right into the middle of my problems and discouragement to meet me there. God wants to be with me every moment of the day to help me face challenges, difficulties, and discouragements. God doesn't want to wait on the sidelines.

When I allow Jesus to step into my life to help and serve others or to heal areas of my life, or when I let Jesus step into the emptiness, messiness, or discouragement in my life, then I give him the freedom to overwhelm me in ways that I would never expect.

Oratio

Jesus, I see you on the shore looking toward me, to see if I have a boat ready for you to jump into if the crowd overwhelms you. I feel unsure at times as you call me to share in your mission. Yet as soon as you set foot in my boat I sense your power and peace flooding my being. A spontaneous "Yes!" escapes my lips. My boat is ready for you!

Contemplatio

"Jesus, come into my boat."

Friday of the Second Week
of Ordinary Time

⋮ · · · · · · · · · · · · ⋮

Lectio

Mark 3:13–19

Meditatio

> *"He appointed Twelve . . . that they might be with him*
> *and he might send them forth . . ."*

As I read this line: "[Jesus] summoned those whom he wanted and they came to him," I imagine a magnetic quality of Jesus, beautifully portrayed in many films such as the *Gospel According to John.* Jesus calls the disciples by name, and they follow. They recognize in Jesus the fulfillment of a desire for fullness of life deep within. I want this too! But I am struck by the apparent tension in the appointment of the Twelve: *called* by God to follow Jesus closely, and also *sent* to go forth. Coming *toward* and sending *out*—this is the apparent tension of all called to discipleship.

It was on the *mountain* that Jesus summoned those he wanted. Like the disciples at Mount Tabor during the Transfiguration, I like being on the mountain. Yet, although I want others to come to know and experience Jesus, I haven't always felt ready for Jesus to send me out, *down the mountain.*

As years pass by, however, I understand more fully the words of the founder of the Pauline family, Blessed James

Alberione, regarding the contemplative and active life. In our call to discipleship, there is no separation between prayer and apostolic activity, being called and being sent. In his thought, an apostle is one who bears God in his or her own soul and radiates God to those all around. The apostle is a temple of the Holy Trinity, exuding God from all his or her pores.

Through our baptism, we are *all* called to holiness and sent to share the Good News. Jesus extends to us the invitation to follow him more closely and to go out to proclaim the word that we have received. We are called to know and live Christ in order to give him to the world in which we live. Called to be *with the Lord* and to *go out* and communicate him—we need both.

Oratio

Jesus, you call me by name and ask that I follow you. It is easy to follow you in moments of closeness . . . harder in moments where I cannot see your presence as clearly, or in moments when what you ask of me seems hard, even impossible.

May I grow in intimacy with you, understanding your heart always more. May I fathom more deeply the unconditional love you have for all people. May I live of your love and be able to communicate you to those around me. Amen.

Contemplatio

Send me, Lord.

Saturday of the Second Week
of Ordinary Time

:· · · · · · · · · · · ·:

Lectio

Mark 3:20–21

Meditatio

"When his relatives heard of this. . . ."

Everyone faces family conflicts. Some erupt quickly and die down just as fast, while others are deep-rooted and long-lasting. Today's Gospel tells us that even Jesus had trouble with his relatives. No wonder he warned us that no prophet is accepted in his hometown, and that one's enemies are of one's own household. In this part of Mark's Gospel, Jesus is establishing a new family, a family of disciples. Yesterday we read about his choice of the Twelve as his apostles. They were the first members of his new family. Today we find that his relatives think he's out of his mind. So they interfere and try to stop him from carrying out his work. Toward the end of this chapter of Mark, Jesus will identify the real members of his family: those who hear the word of God and carry it out. Those who do God's will are the mothers, sisters, and brothers of Jesus.

Jesus' radical demand can force us into making some painful choices. Whom do we put first in our lives, God or our family? The other side of this dilemma is that even if we face rejection from our relatives, Jesus will always accept us. The only condition is to do his will. Doing his will, following his commands, is something that he wants us to do freely, to give the gift of our love. It is not a heavy burden, but an easy yoke. Through baptism we have become disciples of Jesus, members of his family. That is our basic Christian vocation. Within it, we receive a further call to live out our discipleship in a unique way: through marriage, single life, consecrated life, or priesthood. Family conflicts often arise over these vocational choices. Sometimes we have to make choices that our relatives may disapprove of—just as Jesus did. But we do so with the secure knowledge that we are doing the will of God, who will never abandon us.

Oratio

Jesus, sometimes I have conflicts with my family members. You know what this is like, since your own relatives opposed you and didn't understand what you were doing. Despite any disagreements, help me to love my family members just as you loved yours. Help me to do my best to listen to them and understand their point of view, even while putting your will first.

Contemplatio

Jesus, thank you for making me part of your family.

Third Sunday of Ordinary Time —
Year A

∴ · · · · · · · · · · · · ∴

Lectio

Matthew 4:12–23

Meditatio

"Repent, for the kingdom of heaven is at hand."

This phrase marks the beginning of Jesus' public ministry in the Gospels of Matthew and Mark. It is also one of the phrases that can be used during the distribution of ashes on Ash Wednesday. In this crucial phrase, Jesus tells us the key for belonging to the kingdom of heaven on earth: repentance.

Consistent with this Gospel passage is the first post-resurrection exhortation of Peter: "They asked Peter and the other apostles, 'what are we to do, my brothers?' Peter [said] to them, 'Repent and be baptized'" (Acts 2:38).

What is repentance? How do I repent? Saint Paul's experience is probably the best to help us understand just what this call to repentance is. Paul kept the commandments and all the other precepts of the Law according to his own understanding of what God wanted. Jesus called him to repentance on the way to Damascus—to abandon his own understanding for that of Jesus. The Letter to the Ephesians describes this experience: "That is not how you learned Christ, assuming that you have heard of him and were taught in him, as truth is in Jesus, that you should put away the old self of your former way of life, corrupted through deceitful desires, and be renewed in the spirit of your minds, and put on the new self, created in God's way in righteousness and holiness of truth" (4:20–24).

This call invites me to become a follower of Jesus, abandoning my sense of what God wants in order to embrace God's way. It cuts deeply to the heart of my being. Am I a follower of Jesus—a member of the kingdom of heaven? Have I repented of my way of thinking, behaving, saying things, judging? Have I allowed Jesus to renew my mind, search my heart, and motivate my will? Am I still in possession of myself?

Oratio

Jesus, I want to repent and embrace the kingdom of heaven. I struggle to understand what this means. Like Paul, I keep the commandments and try to do what I believe is pleasing to you. May my heart be open to receiving the grace of repentance so that I may truly follow you instead of unconsciously following myself, others, or the ways of the world. May I act as you would act, speak as you would speak, think as you would think, love as you would love. Thus may I find your kingdom once again near at hand in my life and in the lives of all those around me. Amen.

Contemplatio

Jesus, renew my mind; re-create me in your image.

Third Sunday of Ordinary Time —
Year B

∴ · · · · · · · · · · · · ∴

Lectio

Mark 1:14–20

Meditatio

"Come after me . . ."

Today we read about Christ's call to the first four apostles, that is, to two sets of brothers: Simon (who becomes Peter) and his brother Andrew, James and his brother John. In this Gospel, the evangelist Mark gives us a brief snapshot of this event. All four men, fishermen by trade, are working in or around their boats as Jesus passes by. He calls them, and they immediately follow him.

The fascination that surrounds the person of Jesus conquers their hearts. They do not hesitate to follow him. They are leaving behind what is most significant in their lives: their families, homes, and livelihoods. The fishing business of Zebedee, the father of James and John, must have been doing fairly well for him to have hired men.

Jesus still calls disciples today. Those invited to priesthood and religious life feel the call to follow Christ in a life of discipleship, and leave everything behind to follow him. But God's call is not only for priests and religious; it reaches each of us. At some point, Jesus passes through our life and attracts us to him. As it happened with the apostles, Christ usually comes to meet us in the most ordinary places. He called the apostles out of their fishing boats, while they were doing their daily work. He may call me, in the ordinary places of my life, to a deeper relationship with him.

His call often involves sacrifice. Like the four apostles who left family and a lucrative business, I may be invited to let go of things I hold dear. This is the cost of discipleship. But the reward and the joy of being with Christ will far surpass anything I may have forfeited.

Oratio

Lord Jesus, let me be attentive so that I will recognize your call to me. It will probably come in an ordinary time and place. May my heart be fascinated by you, so that I will have the courage to leave what is not necessary for the journey of discipleship, and lovingly follow you by serving others.

Contemplatio

Lord, today I will listen for your call in the ordinariness of my life.

Third Sunday of Ordinary Time — Year C

∴ · · · · · · · · · · · ∵

Lectio

Luke 1:1–4, 4:14–21

Meditatio

"The Spirit of the Lord is upon me . . ."

Today's Gospel involves beginnings: the beginning of the Gospel according to Saint Luke, and the beginning of Jesus' public ministry. Both Luke and Jesus clearly know that they are carrying out a specific mission for the sake of others. Luke writes: "so that you may realize the certainty of the teachings you have received," and Jesus uses the words of the prophet Isaiah to speak about the freedom and new life that his ministry will bring.

At this time of year, near the beginning of our new calendar year and the weeks of Ordinary Time in the Church, it can be helpful to reflect on our own beginnings as well. As Christians, the Holy Spirit came upon us in particularly powerful moments at our Baptism and Confirmation. These are two of the sacraments that initiate our life in Christ and in the Church, so that we, too, can say with Isaiah and with Jesus, "The Spirit of the Lord is upon me . . . ." This anointing of the Spirit does not leave us simply with a gift that makes us feel good, a gift to keep to ourselves. Rather, the gift of the Spirit sends us, as it sent Isaiah, Jesus, and the Gospel writer, to proclaim "glad tidings" and "liberty" with the Good News of the Gospel.

This gift and call that the Holy Spirit extends to us at our Baptism and Confirmation continues into the "today" of our lives, here and now. The Holy Spirit calls each of us to proclaim the Gospel in the midst of the particular family, work, and relationships that make up the fabric of our daily lives. I want to pay attention to the many opportunities the Lord gives me each day to bring "liberty to captives," including listening to others, forgiving those who have hurt me, and comforting those who grieve.

Oratio

Father, Son, and Holy Spirit, one God in three persons, I want to treasure the gift of your presence within me. At my Baptism, you placed your special seal within me and made me your child. I pray that your life in me may flow out to others. Help me to be attentive to your promptings and open to your grace that sends me in love to bring new life, liberty, and joy to the people in my life today.

Contemplatio

". . . the love of God has been poured out into our hearts . . ." (Rom 5:5).

Monday of the Third Week
of Ordinary Time

⁝ · · · · · · · · · · · · ⁝

Lectio

Mark 3:22–30

Meditatio

> *"And if Satan has risen up against himself and is divided,*
> *he cannot stand . . ."*

At first glance, this Gospel passage may appear puzzling. The scribes are making some serious accusations against Jesus—they accuse him of being possessed by the devil himself, and of using Satan's power to drive out evil spirits. Jesus responds through a series of analogies and parables, but what does he mean? Are his words still relevant today?

The answer is a resounding yes! Jesus takes the accusations of his adversaries and uses them to proclaim the arrival of God's kingdom. He points out that if he is truly working to drive out Satan by using Satan's own power against him, then it means that Satan's kingdom is divided from within and cannot last. But if the hands of this strong adversary are tied, then it means a stronger power has arrived—a power that has already conquered the enemy and foiled his plot. In either case, Satan is defeated and God is victorious in Christ.

Jesus' words leave me wondering about the kingdom of my own heart. So often, I have admired the "undivided heart" and great focus of the saints. They never take their gaze off Christ! Nothing deters or distracts them, so they find their hearts at peace, even in the midst of great trials. As I watch Jesus today, I can't help but compare his response with my own. Jesus is being falsely accused before a large crowd of people, yet he doesn't react with anger or defensiveness. Rather than perceiving a threat, Jesus perceives an *opportunity*—a teaching moment in his ministry. Nothing distracts him from the Father, nor from his own mission of love.

Today, Jesus brings us Good News. Because of Jesus' power, Satan's kingdom is falling down around him. Jesus, the "Stronger One," is here to plunder Satan's property, and to take full possession of every heart. We have only to surrender and cooperate with this awesome grace.

Oratio

Jesus, your words and actions in today's Gospel fill me with hope. Help me to see the opportunities that lie behind moments of challenge and confrontation. Ground me so deeply in your love that, rather than reacting in haste and anger, I am able to see the needs of those before me, especially their need for your light and your love. Jesus, you have already conquered sin and death—I offer you my own heart as well. Conquer me, Lord! May all that I am belong to you. Allow me to be so mesmerized by your beauty and truth that my gaze remains fixed on you unwaveringly.

Contemplatio

Jesus, help me to keep my gaze fixed on you!

Tuesday of the Third Week
of Ordinary Time

⁙ · · · · · · · · · · · · ⁙

Lectio

Mark 3:31–35

Meditatio

> *". . . looking around at those seated in the circle . . ."*

In Jesus' day, disciples sat at the feet of their rabbi or teacher. This indicated that the disciples recognized the authority of the rabbi or teacher and were ready to listen and to learn.

Picture this scene. Crowding one another a bit, people sit around Jesus, listening to him, as he teaches and forms them. As people praying with Scripture, we too are sitting at his feet, attentive to his word. Jesus looks around the circle and sees each person, pausing to make eye contact with each individual. He refers to all those around him as mother, sister, and brother. These words are just as powerful today as they were two thousand years ago.

Since we too sit at his feet, he is also calling us mother, sister, and brother. These are not arbitrary titles. Jesus is calling us a real family. He lets us know that he is our actual brother, a brother who protects and a brother who loves. He looks at us and invites us to see ourselves truly as his brother, his sister, his mother—in short, to see ourselves as his family.

This can be hard to fully accept when we acknowledge the ways and times in which we have sinned. In fact, we may even feel like hanging our heads in shame and walking away from the invitation. But as Jesus gazes at us and calls us to be family, he does so fully knowing our sinfulness. He still calls us to be his family.

Interestingly, this invitation is twofold. Jesus looks around the circle and calls you and me to be his family *and* to be family to one another. For if we are truly—not just in name—Jesus' mother, brother, and sister, then we are also mother, brother, and sister to one another. The gift of this Gospel is the gift of a close family relationship with God as well as an enlarged family—the gift of each other.

Oratio

Today, I place myself at your feet, Lord. Give me the grace that I need this day to remain at your feet and not turn away from your gaze. I want to listen to your truth and learn to walk in your way. Then I want to follow you who give life to me and all my brothers and sisters. As I go about the activities that will fill this day, may I find and truly see the mothers, brothers, and sisters you have given me. Amen.

Contemplatio

You are my mother, brother, and sister.

Wednesday of the Third Week
of Ordinary Time

⟨··············⟩

Lectio

Mark 4:1–20

Meditatio

"On one occasion, Jesus began to teach by the sea."

I can hear the waves lapping gently against the shore as Jesus gets into the boat, finding a place to sit down. He faces the crowd that waits expectantly along the water's edge. I let the sound of the water calm me. I can see and hear him better from his place in the boat.

Jesus wants me to hear him, and there, on the sea, he begins to speak about just that. "Hear this!" He uses a parable that centers on the word of God as a seed. In some it yields thirtyfold, in some sixtyfold, and in some even a hundredfold. He also speaks of those who *look and see* but do not perceive.

I want to hear, to see, to understand, and I feel the deep importance of grasping Jesus' words. Parables are like riddles. I want to wrestle with the riddle that Jesus presents to me in this story about the sower. Anyone who has struggled to crack open a challenging riddle knows that one's whole being becomes tuned to the terms used in the riddle, the possibilities, and the ultimate meaning it promises to unfold. One's attention is rapt, hooked hopelessly until the meaning is clear.

Jesus wants me to be just that intent, even more, on him and his kingdom. His word and his parables hold such a depth of life-giving meaning that they infuse my life with a mysterious joy. What will root me more firmly in this word? If I find myself choking on some aspect of the word, do I bring it to the Lord? Do I lay down before him my difficulties with the word? I can ask him how he wants to work through this word in my life today. I know that he wants to bear fruit through me. What one thing can I do today to work with him to produce abundantly?

Oratio

Jesus, you want me to hear and understand you, and your desire for me to "get it" drives you to do whatever it takes to break through my deafness. I'm not always so awake or attentive. My weakness is not important, because *you* never give up. Thank you for that, Lord. I want to pay attention to what the day brings me, and to see you working in my life. Help me see how your word shines light on this day. You are most assuredly present with me! I embrace you now and throughout this day by acknowledging the many hidden ways you touch me. I believe.

Contemplatio

"Whoever has ears to hear ought to hear."

Thursday of the Third Week of Ordinary Time

∴ · · · · · · · · · · · · ∴

Lectio

Mark 4:21–25

Meditatio

". . . more will be given . . ."

If you don't use it, you lose it. This is often said about speaking a foreign language, practicing an art, or using other skills. The gift remains, but the ability to use it is impaired or lost. So it is with spiritual insight. It's not that *God* takes the gift away; it just rusts out.

Faith is both a gift or power to believe and the "habit" of believing. With it comes a certain knack in perceiving the meaning of God's word. While the lamp in today's Gospel refers to the parable Jesus related in yesterday's reading, it also refers to this spiritual sixth sense. Jesus' parables were designed to illumine, not shroud, the word of God. So too, our response of faith in life can be a light to others. Everything will become fully clear at the final coming of Christ. Meanwhile, the word is to be personally deepened, and "broadcast" to others like the seed in yesterday's parable.

How can faith and its fruit grow so that they "remain" (a key word in John 15)? In that chapter Jesus talks about the faith relationship and how the taking away involves pruning. Sometimes we believers hesitate to share what we believe or how Jesus influences our lives. We feel we lack the right words, or are afraid we won't know how to respond to challenges or ridicule.

Jesus says today that the more we share, the more firmly we'll believe. Our skills will be sharpened. In listening to Jesus and acting on his word, we lend credibility to what we say about him or do in his name. Conversely, in sharing his life and word with others, we grow in our own faith and develop our ability, given to us at Baptism, to be his witnesses. We won't be perfect. We'll sometimes be hobbled by doubts and even sin. But by committing ourselves to prayer for this grace, we will put ourselves in God's hands to be a light for others and give them hope.

Oratio

Lord, I've noticed that what helps others is not always what I share with them in the blazing light of glorious faith, but in its darkness, as you tell us in tomorrow's Gospel . . . and as happened when you died: "Truly this man was the Son of God!" (Mk 15:39). Let my life, hidden and lackluster as it often seems, give someone else a reason to believe and the desire to belong to you. Let them hear from me an echo of your word to them.

Contemplatio

Jesus, be my light and make me a light for others.

Friday of the Third Week
of Ordinary Time

✣············✣

Lectio

Mark 4:26–34

Meditatio

". . . the seed would sprout and grow, he knows not how."

Today's Gospel follows closely on the parable of the sower. The two stories share a common thread: the inexorable growth of the kingdom. It's thought that Mark wrote his Gospel for Christians in Rome who had been undergoing persecution. When the word was proclaimed at their gatherings, this passage about God-given increase must have encouraged them. The marvelous germination of seeds and growth of shoots recalls the action of grace and invites Christians to hope in God's ultimate triumph over evil.

Listening to Mark's Gospel again and again as the years passed, Rome's Christians must have taken courage from this Galilean parable of a growth that could not be slowed or halted. The parable implies that through the action of the Holy Spirit the ultimate victory will belong to Christ and the Church.

During the coming weeks, Mark's Gospel will show us Jesus' humanness and his sufferings. It's thought that Mark intended this emphasis to further encourage the persecuted:

Jesus, although divine, manifested human weaknesses and underwent all forms of unjust treatment—from betrayal, to an unfair trial, to a criminal's death. The disciple should not think himself or herself better than the Master. But with God's grace the disciple can prevail, even if he or she has to pay the ultimate price.

Centuries of martyrs have borne witness to God's powerful grace. Grace can make even the weakest of human beings heroic. After the genocide in Rwanda, Immaculée Ilibagiza found the inner strength to forgive the neighbors who had murdered most of her family and would have slain her, too, had they found her. Immaculée's story is one of many such from the twentieth century and opening years of the twenty-first.

Grace can transform the world.

Oratio

Jesus, help me to understand this era in which we live—a time between your first and second comings, when we are called to work out our salvation, as Saint Paul said (see Phil 2:12), with the help of your grace. May the images of seed, shoot, blade, ear, and ripe grain give me hope and courage. May green, growing things remind me of the presence and power of your Spirit, making all things new.

Contemplatio

Lord, I can do all things in you who give me strength.

Saturday of the Third Week of Ordinary Time

∶⋯⋯⋯⋯⋯⋰

Lectio

Mark 4:35–41

Meditatio

"Why are you terrified?"

We have sat with Jesus and his disciples in the boat since Wednesday, listening to him speak in images and parables: the sower and the seed (Wednesday), the lamp on a lamp stand (Thursday), the ripe grain and the mustard seed (Friday). Today, even as we're still puzzling over the meaning of what he has just said, he tells the disciples to cross over to the other shore. Meanwhile, he promptly falls asleep after a full day of teaching. It seems as though the disciples are left to their own devices to deal with the details of the real world, which become nasty in a matter of seconds. They panic and wake him up.

The disciples' prayer is raw and uncensored. "Teacher, do you not care that we are perishing?" I may not use those exact words, but I know about that prayer. Sometimes it simply comes out as a straightforward "help." Once in a while it sounds more like "HELP NOW!"

"Why are you terrified? Do you not yet have faith?"

Well, yes I have faith . . . but sometimes—quite often, actually—it gets a little thin. I know in my mind that Jesus can do all things. I know that God's love is unconditional and works everything out for the best in the long run. At least in theory all this is clear to me. In practice, however, it's another story. Real life easily blows out of control. While I'm still trying to make sense of information and circumstances, decisions need to be made, actions cannot be put off. Like the disciples, I cast off and cross over to the other shore as best I can. And then come the unforeseen conditions and consequences—a thousand and one variables all shifting and tossing like a sea churned up in a storm. I panic because I know life is out of my control, and I forget that ultimately God, a loving and wise Father, is in control.

Oratio

Lord, I believe. Help dissipate my unbelief! I know that you are Lord of sea and sky, the past and the future. Everything unknown and out of my control is apparent to you. My adventures into life's unchartered waters easily turn into times of heightened anxiety, if not downright terror. When that happens, Lord, may I *always* turn to you with my honest prayer, as raw and uncensored as it may be. May I always be open to hearing your voice remind me once again to have faith in you.

Contemplatio

Do not be afraid. I am with you.

Fourth Sunday of Ordinary Time — Year A

∵ ⋯⋯⋯ ∴

Lectio

Matthew 5:1–12a

Meditatio

"Blessed are they who hunger and thirst for righteousness. . . ."

What do you most want in life? A cruise? A college education for your children? A larger home? Another car? A safe delivery for your daughter's baby? A good night's sleep?

At any moment we have some desire or need uppermost in our minds and prayers. When we hear Jesus proclaim the poor, the meek, the lowly, and the clean of heart blessed, we may cringe a bit. We could say, *After all, I need these things; I deserve them; I've worked hard for them.* But we separate ourselves from Jesus' hearty embrace when we see our desires in opposition to what he is proclaiming in the Beatitudes.

A way forward through this impasse lies in the beatitude: "Blessed are they who hunger and thirst for righteousness. . . ." This beatitude is interwoven with the promises in Isaiah that the everlasting covenant made with David would be transferred to the people (see Is 55:3–5), a promise that God would restore the people to freedom and prosperity.

The Jewish people at the time of Jesus were oppressed and impoverished. They too had desires, many of them for security, power, or freedom, the same life and death issues we deal with daily. Jesus came along to gather up all our desires and fulfill them, often in ways we wouldn't expect. At the bottom of every earthly desire lurks something authentic, something true, a spark of the desire for the eternal banquet of heaven, everlasting happiness. In the Beatitudes, Jesus is saying, "Look, that moment is here. What you have been waiting for is here. I am here. The kingdom is here and now. I will fulfill all your longings and so much more if you depend entirely on me."

The mysteries of life and death have been planted in deeper soil since Jesus walked among us. In our joy we plant the seed of our earthly desires in the soil of the eternal faithfulness of God, trusting that in every way he will carry us toward what we most authentically desire.

Oratio

In every event of my life and that of my family, Lord, I desire holiness for each of us. I trust in your faithfulness to us always, that in everything, the bitter and the sweet, you will in some way bring us closer to eternal bliss. Amen.

Contemplatio

I desire you, Lord. I long for your kingdom.

Fourth Sunday of Ordinary Time —
Year B

∴ · · · · · · · · · · · ∴

Lectio

Mark 1:21–28

Meditatio

"I know who you are."

Has it ever happened that someone you thought you knew well did something that truly surprised you? Something out of character? Something that made you say: "I didn't know she had it in her?"

The demon in today's Gospel claims to know Jesus. But does it really know who Jesus is? Perhaps the demon is trying to flatter Jesus, to pretend to give him homage, in a vain attempt to curry his favor. Jesus rebukes the demon and demands that it come out of the possessed man. And the demon has no choice but to obey. The exorcism of the demon falls between two of Mark's comments about the teaching of Jesus. Mark first reports that the people are astonished at Jesus' teaching, for he taught with authority. Then, after the demon is cast out, the people marvel, "What is this? A new teaching with authority."

In his teaching, Jesus instructs us about God. We may think we know who God is. But do we really? In early life we may absorb ideas about God that give us a distorted image of him. Even when we know from our faith, for example, that God loves us, we may find it hard to actually believe that. We may harbor the idea that God is a severe taskmaster, always watching for some mistake we make in order to punish us for it.

Just as Jesus cast out the demon, he can cast out from our minds these distorted ideas. He will do that when we go before him in faith and ask him to teach us who God is, to show us the Father. Prayerfully reading the Gospels will gradually form our minds in the truth about God. Then we will be able to say truthfully, "I know who you are."

Oratio

Lord Jesus, come and show yourself to me. Cast out from my mind any false ideas I may have about who you are, and who your Father is. When we know you, we will also know the Father. I want to learn from you and to trust in your love. When I am tempted to doubt your love and mercy, cast those fears away from me and fill me instead with loving confidence.

Contemplatio

Jesus, I believe in your love.

Fourth Sunday of Ordinary Time — Year C

⋰⋯⋯⋯⋰

Lectio

Luke 4:21–30

Meditatio

> *"Isn't this the son of Joseph?"*

I'm trying to understand the townspeople's reaction to Jesus by recalling my own hometown community. Although I was amazed and delighted when one of my high school's graduates became a best-selling author, I think I'd have been incredulous if any of the Donalds, Ronalds, Marilyns, or Judiths in my own class had become famous in any way. We knew one another too well to envision fame. We were ordinary.

I think Jesus' fellow townsfolk felt that he, too, was ordinary. What was he doing—after a few months' absence—returning home to stand up in the synagogue and speak with authority? A workman who claimed that he was fulfilling a prophecy of Isaiah! And referring to Gentiles as if they were on an equal footing with Nazarenes? No way! Relatives and neighbors couldn't accept this "new" Jesus.

Meanwhile, in other towns and villages, Jesus was attracting people. It had to be his personality, more than his miracles, that drew them. According to John's Gospel, the temple guards said that no one had ever spoken like Jesus (see Jn 8:46).

Before he left Nazareth to preach and heal, Jesus may have seemed much like the other young men of his town. Was he taller than average? He's usually portrayed that way, unlike Paul, whose very name means "small." But how can we know for sure? During his adolescence and young adulthood, might Jesus have seemed completely average?

Reflecting on this makes me wonder about the ordinary-looking people in my own life. Perhaps some of them (family members, friends, coworkers, and acquaintances) are actually leading lives of great holiness. Judgment Day may hold some real surprises! This is one more motive for treating everyone with more respect and kindness.

Oratio

Jesus, I can't help wondering what you were like during your teens and twenties. It's hard to think of you as ordinary, but you must have seemed so to your relatives and neighbors. I wonder if there are people whom I know—men, women, or children—who seem ordinary, yet are really living lives of great devotion, virtue, and even heroism. This is a reason for me to try to see you in everyone who crosses my path. Your hidden life is intriguing and mysterious, whether in Nazareth or on my own street!

Contemplatio

Who's in our midst?

Monday of the Fourth Week
of Ordinary Time

⁝⋯⋯⋯⋯⋯⋮

Lectio

Mark 5:1–20

Meditatio

"And they were seized with fear."

This Gospel reading is perhaps one of the most dramatic, but also one of the most tragic. We are told about the man possessed by a whole legion of evil spirits. His conduct certainly bears this out. For years he has broken out of every attempt to keep him subdued. He could be seen running around the hills screaming and injuring himself. We imagine the townspeople have made every effort to avoid him; they have warned their children to stay away from the area he inhabits. His wildness is seen as a threat to all. As soon as Jesus and the disciples disembark, the man races to meet them—not out of joy, but out of compulsion. His inner demons know the true identity of Jesus. Evil cannot stand good.

The man confronts Jesus, knowing that Jesus has power over him. "Don't torment me. Leave me be." As the man is pleading, Jesus is overpowering the demons. "Go out of him," he commands. Evil always wants the last word, so the demons suggest a compromise. "Send us into the swine." Jesus complies, and the entire herd goes mad and runs into the sea to drown. This side note might strike us as unjust. Someone's livelihood has been destroyed. Why would Christ not send the demons back to hell and leave the swine in peace? First, the Jews were forbidden to eat swine, which was considered unclean. Perhaps the people raising the swine were Jews. If so, Jesus has just eliminated their impediment to following the Law. Second, Jesus only gave the demons permission to enter the swine; he did not send them into the swine.

All of this makes for great drama, but what should have been cause for rejoicing turns tragic. When the townspeople see the man they had feared now sitting calm and coherent, they beg Jesus to leave their territory. Because they do not understand what just happened, they fear it. Not every marvel of grace is recognized and accepted.

Oratio

Jesus, Lord of heaven and earth, you are the center of such power and mercy! Sometimes you bless us with an unmistakable wonder of grace. More often you work little marvels in my life, within my family and among my friends. Keep me alert. Keep me humble before you. Give me an open and grateful heart, always anticipating your every word and work. May I have eyes to recognize your gift, a tongue to praise you, a heart to love you, and a will to imitate you. Amen.

Contemplatio

"Go home and tell everyone what God in his mercy has done for you."

Tuesday of the Fourth Week of Ordinary Time

⋰⋰⋰⋰⋰⋰⋰⋰

Lectio

Mark 5:21–43

Meditatio

> *". . . your faith has saved you."*

These words highlight for me Jesus' delicacy and attention for women, an attitude not often noted in the times in which he lived. I think of the Chinese saying, "Women hold up half the sky," and am filled with gratitude that the Savior was a true gentleman. The woman to whom Jesus speaks is afflicted with an embarrassing and debilitating disorder, a flow of blood that also renders her unclean. By searching for her, Jesus indicates that he is not satisfied with her anonymous cure. It seems that he wants to look into her eyes and call her "daughter," to remind her of the dignity of her nature and his deep regard for all women.

Jesus then moves on to the distraught father of a little girl who is dying, and they receive news of her death. Jesus asks the father to have faith, and when they arrive at his home, the father's faith is rewarded. Jesus calmly calls the little girl back to life with that precious phrase preserved for all time in his own language: "*Talitha koum*," which means, "Little girl, I say to you, arise!"

It is a challenging day for Jesus. He has to put up with impatience from his disciples and ridicule from the mourners of the little girl. But Jesus pays them scant attention. It is clear that he is absorbed in relieving the suffering of two groups who have always been the most vulnerable in society: women and girls. Jesus' respect for women will not go away, enshrined as it is in the Gospels. To women, it brings strength and renewal, and to men, a reminder of where greatness truly lies.

Oratio

Jesus, your gentle respect moves me very deeply and reaffirms me in a way I find hard to express. Help me to be open to your grace, so that I can remember to carry your respect and regard to every person I meet—man, woman, or child. I trust that I will then be like you, bringing healing and hope wherever I go.

Contemplatio

"Do not be afraid; just have faith."

Wednesday of the Fourth Week
of Ordinary Time

⁚ · · · · · · · · · · · ⁚

Lectio

Mark 6:1–6

Meditatio

> *"So he was not able to perform any mighty deed there . . ."*

Much is happening in this short Gospel passage. Jesus is preaching in his native area and the people are astonished at his wisdom. They even marvel at the miracles he has performed, yet they take offense at him. They have the attitude, "Who does he think he is?" They talk to one another about his human origins, but they don't talk to Jesus himself. They don't ask *him* why he can do things only God can do. They have closed their minds to the possibility that God has come among them in human form. They see the miracles but refuse to see their meaning. They hear the truth, but do not heed the words.

They have become too familiar with what they have heard of his family and the ordinary circumstances of his upbringing in their small town. They reject the possibility that there is more to the story of his life than they know, so they are blind to the revelation of who Jesus is. They let who they *think* Jesus is limit their openness to who he *really* is.

"So he was not able to perform any mighty deed there." It wasn't that he couldn't cure them—as Son of the eternal Father he certainly had the power to do so. But this is how God chooses to work. He gives us the gift of free will so that we may use it to cooperate in our own salvation and healing. He offers his love and healing but never forces us to accept it, for he wills that we respond in love and faith. Love isn't love if it isn't freely given. God reveals himself to us in so many ways throughout the day—it is up to us to keep our eyes and hearts open so we can understand what he is saying to us.

Oratio

Lord, let me never close my eyes to your loving mercy or close my ears to your truth. Help me to understand what you are trying to say to me as I meditate on your word. I know that you can do all things, wonderful things, even in me— poor sinner that I am. Help me to see you in those around me and to believe that you *can* and *want to* work great marvels of grace in them, too. Give them also the grace to be open to you.

Contemplatio

Open my eyes that I may see you, Lord.

Thursday of the Fourth Week of Ordinary Time

⁝ · · · · · · · · · · · · ⁝

Lectio

Mark 6:7–13

Meditatio

> *"Jesus . . . began to send them out two by two. . . ."*

I sometimes wonder if Jesus really knew what he was doing when he sent the disciples out two by two. In so doing he created the model for mission until the end of the ages. I wonder if he could foresee the arguments between parish board members, competition and jealousy in religious communities, embarrassing disagreements among the clergy. These things always make me cringe. At the most the interplay of relationships gone awry in ecclesial circles is a source of scandal, and at the very least it is a cause of frustration. Wouldn't we be free to spread the Gospel in peace if we could each just do our own thing? Think how much more good could be done.

But what if these relationships are actually a central part of announcing the Gospel, rather than simply the way in which it is done? This passage doesn't speak only of the disciples going forth in pairs. They are also told to seek hospitality in someone's home and to stay there until they leave the area. They are to preach to others a message that deeply touches their personal lives, bringing them into profound contact with others. And they cure the sick by laying their hands on them. These activities lift up the four virtues of interdependence, hospitality, truth-telling, and healing, all of which require encounters among people.

If Jesus had set up a model of apostolic entrepreneurs, probably a lot of creative ideas would have resulted in projects carried out efficiently. However, egoism and individualism would have marred the message. Instead, with the law of "two by two," humility, simplicity, reconciliation, and love must be practiced and not primarily preached. Perhaps *this* is the message.

It is undoubtedly, then, a mistake to push issues of relationship and community-building aside in order to get on with announcing the Gospel, or the building project in the parish, or the mission in a community. How we get along *is* the message.

Oratio

Jesus, my Lord, I cannot do great things for you. I ask you, though, to help me do what is often the hardest thing of all: to get along with others, to let another have the last word, to look out for what makes another happy, to give in. In this way I will be confident that I too am a missionary in the world today. Amen.

Contemplatio

"We should love one another" (I Jn 3:11).

Friday of the Fourth Week of Ordinary Time

∴ · · · · · · · · · · · · ∴

Lectio

Mark 6:14–29

Meditatio

"The king was deeply distressed . . ."

I imagine myself in King Herod's banquet hall, watching the servants scurry about, attending to the guests' every need. As I read this passage, I find it distasteful but I stick with it, hoping that I will be open enough to welcome what the Lord wants to teach me.

Previously, the Baptizer had admonished Herod for his unlawful behavior. He spoke these words in goodness and truth, hoping that Herod would change. Herod felt attracted to John's words, and even though he was "much perplexed . . . he liked to listen to him." The Spirit was stirring things up in Herod's heart and pointing to deeper realities. Would Herod listen?

Then sadly, I see that tonight Herod does not follow the path of God. Instead, he veers off into fear and, despite being "deeply distressed," chooses to please the crowd. I, too, am distressed. What might have been if Herod had chosen otherwise? And my choices today, will they be for life? For goodness? Or will I live out of fear and crowd-pleasing?

Herod was deeply distressed. God was knocking at the door of his heart, his conscience. To come to awareness, to be stirred to remorse, is a sign that the Spirit is working in one's heart. It is a gift and a grace, to be welcomed. Even in the case of great sin, it is a messenger sent by God to wake us up and call us back. I can refuse it and let in a world that sleeps in death, or I can accept it, embrace it, and walk past my fear to a greater and fuller life. It is a great blessing to be moved to distress, for it is the Lord calling out to us.

Oratio

Lord, I thank you for working in my life and that of others. Help me to pay attention to your movements within me. Help me to live in your light. I pray, too, for my fellow travelers on this journey of life. If I find someone in distress today, let me listen carefully and through my words and actions help that person follow your way. Give us all courage to listen and to overcome our fears so that we can become men and women who, in a fallen world, give hope.

Contemplatio

You are a shield to all who take refuge in you!

Saturday of the Fourth Week of Ordinary Time

∴· · · · · · · · · · · ·∴

Lectio

Mark 6:30–34

Meditatio

> *". . . his heart was moved with pity for them . . ."*

Today's liturgy reveals the compassionate heart of Christ, our Master and Shepherd. The apostles are returning home after their first apostolic trip, when Jesus sent them to preach, teach, and heal the sick. Now they are returning, tired but enthusiastic, eager to share with Jesus all that they have experienced during these first days of ministry. How delighted Jesus is as he listens to their accounts of casting out demons and anointing and healing the sick.

He notices their fatigue after these long days away, for he invites them to come away with him and rest. Jesus cares about their health and all the details of their lives, as he does for each of us. But do I really believe this? Do I believe that he is interested in the details of my day, in the challenges that I face each and every day of my life? Yet this is precisely what this Gospel text is telling me. Jesus is interested! He waits eagerly to hear from me, to spend time with me, so he crosses the lake in order to find this time and space.

Yet on the lake's far shore a "surprise" awaits Jesus, and perhaps me, too. The time and space that we had sought together are not to be found this day, for the needy crowd is waiting for him. They are longing to see Jesus, to hear his words and to be healed by his presence. With his compassionate heart Jesus responds to their need.

Perhaps on this particular day Jesus wants to show me, to teach me to what extent love must go. It does not seek its own comfort, its own convenience, but instead gives of itself to the fullest. It does not focus on its own need, but rather on the needs and cares of others. Am I ready to accept the challenge?

Oratio

Jesus, through your life and example you teach me how to love, and show me to what extent that love must go. You did not stop when, tired and hungry, you desired some quiet time with your disciples. You instead reached out to the crowd in their need, giving yourself to the fullest. Show me how to do this in my own life. Teach me always to respond with compassion to my brothers and sisters.

Contemplatio

Jesus, compassionate and great of heart, make my heart like yours!

Fifth Sunday of Ordinary Time —
Year A

∴· · · · · · · · · · · ·∴

Lectio

Matthew 5:13–16

Meditatio

> *". . . your light must shine before others . . ."*

Yes, I want to shine. "Shining" makes me feel good about myself, boosts my sense of being "someone," and gives me the impression of being important, worthwhile, and of value. But when it is the "I" that shines, that good feeling doesn't last very long. It fades away, leaving me with a gnawing emptiness and disillusionment. And what about the people around me? Are their lives enriched by the shining "me"?

Jesus offers me an alternative. It is as though he says, "The Father made you to shine, but with *his* light. The real light in you comes from him." So much darkness shrouds the world, but the Father has given us his own light, Jesus Christ! Jesus shines in us with an incredible brightness. But the "I" must get out of the way so that Jesus, the light in me, can have room to shine. Here, finally, my need to feel important and to be of value finds its true and lasting fulfillment. The Father trusts me so much that he puts his light in me in the hope that I will let it shine.

When *his* light shines in me, people identify it right away. They see my good deeds and glorify my heavenly Father. Something in them changes. Their hearts are touched and turn toward God because of what they have witnessed. The Father's light in me is meant to be shared with everyone.

How bright is his light in me? Can others see it easily, or do they have to squint to catch a glimpse? What prevents me from letting it shine? Can I identify this light in others? What impact does it have on me?

Oratio

Heavenly Father, it's so easy to take light for granted in our highly technological, electronic world. I often think of the power of light when I walk into a dark church and see the small flickering red candle that signals your presence in the tabernacle. *Your light* is hope, comfort, and strength. And that very light dwells in me. Help me to overcome the hesitation or indifference that blocks your light from shining in me. May all who see me today catch a glimpse of your light and experience a little hope for their journey.

Contemplatio

"In your light we see light" (Ps 36:10).

Fifth Sunday of Ordinary Time — Year B

∴ · · · · · · · · · · · · ∵

Lectio

Mark 1:29–39

Meditatio

> *"He approached . . . and helped her up."*

Today's Gospel impresses us with Jesus' compassion. We observe that as soon as he enters the house of Simon and Andrew, people tell Jesus that Simon's mother-in-law is sick with a fever. He approaches her, helps her up and heals her.

In the evening, everyone in town comes to see Jesus. We can imagine their hope as they bring their ill or possessed family members and neighbors, pleading with Jesus to heal them. We can almost hear the compassion and goodness in his voice, see the gestures as his mercy reaches out to them. His heart is so moved with love that he cures many people suffering from various diseases and drives out many demons.

The following morning, Jesus' compassion leads him to travel to other villages, to preach in those places too. His ministry was not limited to physical healings but was extended to the spiritual. Familiar with Jesus' teachings in the Gospels, we recognize that he instructed and offered guidance and hope to those suffering from confusion, ignorance, sinful behavior, disillusionment, and anguish of heart. Jesus' words were grace-filled and effective. They reached the minds and hearts of his listeners and bore fruit. People's lives were changed by the preaching of Jesus. This may have happened quickly or been more gradual, but it happened.

As we ponder Jesus' compassion in action, we might ask ourselves "What do *we* need healed?" Are we experiencing weakness or some affliction of body or spirit? Are we ignorant or confused? Are we having a hard time overcoming sinful behavior? Are we discouraged? In what way do we need Jesus to approach and help us up?

We turn to him with trust and hope, knowing that we can always count on Jesus' compassion. He continues to instruct and heal, and he wills to do this for us today. Let us pause to identify what help we need today and present this to Jesus.

Oratio

Jesus, as I ponder your compassion I am filled with hope. You healed physical and spiritual infirmities, cast out demons, and preached the Good News. Sometimes I neglect to turn to you for grace and healing. In fact, there are times when I don't even think of you but try to practice virtue and solve problems on my own. Enable me to believe more deeply in your goodness and mercy. Strengthen my trust in you so that I turn to you in every situation. I have these special needs today. . . . With confidence I entrust them to your care.

Contemplatio

I turn to you, Jesus, for healing, light, and grace.

Fifth Sunday of Ordinary Time — Year C

❖· · · · · · · · · · · ·❖

Lectio

Luke 5:1–11

Meditatio

". . . they caught a great number of fish and their nets were tearing."

It has been almost an ordinary day for some fishermen washing their nets. Now they are dead tired. Working hard all night, they have caught absolutely nothing. A large crowd is gathering, pushing and jostling one another, straining to hear the voice of the young preacher standing on the shore of the lake. To protect himself from being crushed and to be able to project his voice to the crowd, Jesus steps into one of the two boats moored by the beach—the boat belonging to Simon, the fisherman. It was unusual for someone to just board a boat and ask the owner to shove off and weigh anchor, but Peter does as the Master requests. Jesus sits down and begins teaching.

When he finishes, Jesus turns to Peter and instructs him to go to deeper water and cast the nets. The request does not seem very promising. Peter hesitates. It does not make sense; they had worked all night . . . but then, he and his crew cast their nets. In a moment the nets are so full they begin tearing. Peter and his partners strain to haul in the unbelievably enormous amount of fish. They fill two boats to the point of sinking!

Astonished and awestruck, Peter falls to his knees and begs the Master to depart from him, a sinful man. He is overcome in the evident presence of divine power. Jesus does not disagree with Peter's assessment of his sinfulness; somehow the Master can work with such a forthright man. He looks at Peter with love and says, "Do not be afraid; from now on you will be catching men." Do not be afraid, Peter. My mercy is unfathomable, superabundant. The miraculous catch of fish is a small sign of what you will do from now on.

Oratio

Lord, human weakness, failure, and sinfulness call forth your supreme generosity in this Gospel story: total self-giving to the multitudes; a miracle for those who had not asked for one but trusted your word; mercy in calling sinful men to intimacy with you in your plan of salvation. I am, dear Lord, like Peter and his companions, a recipient of your abundant love. My seemingly ordinary days with their ordinary actions and events are where you break into my life with your divine surprises! In loving and forgiving me, my God, you absolutely hold nothing back! Today I will take time to remember your mercy and goodness and respond in trust when you request something of me.

Contemplatio

If you say so, Lord, I will do it. Have mercy on me, a sinner.

Monday of the Fifth Week
of Ordinary Time

∴· · · · · · · · · · · ·∴

Lectio

Mark 6:53–56

Meditatio

> *". . . as many as touched it were healed."*

The secret is out: this Jesus can heal people. In the chaotic scene, everyone wants to see Jesus. I once saw something similar at a Mass celebrated by a charismatic priest who had a healing ministry. Crowds milled about outside the large auditorium where Mass would be held, waiting for the doors to be opened. When they were finally unlocked, the crowd literally rushed into the building. Others helped people who were in wheelchairs or on crutches. Something like that happens to Jesus when he appears on this scene. People flock around him just wanting to be healed. We can imagine anxious relatives carrying the sick on mats, or fathers carrying children on their shoulders.

Mark says that people begged Jesus just to let them touch the tassel on his cloak. The word here translated as begged—*parakalein*—literally means "to call to one's side." The word "Paraclete" or Consoler derives from the same root. Mark is presenting Jesus as an advocate for the sick, as their consoler, as the one who comes to their side and makes them whole. Jesus' power is so great that it flows out from him even when people just touch the tassel on his cloak.

They were healed not just because they touched the tassel, but because of their faith. Jesus always made it clear that he can only heal us if we have faith. And the distance of the centuries does nothing to dim our faith. It doesn't matter that we can't meet Jesus in person as the people of his own day did. We can still touch him through faith.

Our contact with Jesus through faith can happen anywhere, anytime. All we need to do is turn our minds and our hearts to Jesus and tell him we believe in him. Then we can ask for whatever we need. Jesus' healing touch involves a complete healing of the person, not just physically, but in mind and heart as well. The ultimate healing is from sin, the only thing that can separate us from God.

Oratio

Jesus, I believe in you. Increase my faith. I know that whenever I turn to you with trust, healing power goes out from you. It is just as powerful today as when you walked among the crowds, going to the side of anyone who called out to you. Jesus, I open my heart to you. Heal me and strengthen me to follow you every day of my life.

Contemplatio

Jesus, heal my heart.

Tuesday of the Fifth Week of Ordinary Time

∴ · · · · · · · · · · · ∴

Lectio

Mark 7:1–13

Meditatio

> *"This people honors me with their lips,*
> *but their hearts are far from me."*

As Catholics, some of us may find Jesus' seeming condemnation of tradition in this passage startling. After all, he is using strong language that causes us to look within our own hearts. We, too, have many traditions. And we, too, can give these a false preeminence in our lives and hearts.

Nonetheless, it is important that we don't miss the point. Jesus is not condemning tradition as such. When properly used and understood, traditions can help us to become increasingly aware of invisible spiritual realities around us. Jesus *is* condemning the practice of empty worship. Are our traditions leading us closer to God and deeper into relationship with him and with others? Or have they become empty lip service—worship separated from true relationship with God and with others?

If we are offering true worship, then our worship will be backed by loving action and relationship. It will have a direct influence on the way we choose to live our daily lives. And we will not allow this to make us feel more important in our own eyes or the eyes of others.

How easy it can be to fall into trying to "prove" our worthiness through what we do! Yet, ultimately, the greatest commandment is to ". . . love the Lord, your God, with all your heart, with all your being, with all your strength, and with all your mind, and your neighbor as yourself" (Lk 10:27). In the end, living our Catholic faith is about ongoing relationship. Our worth comes from being created and loved into existence by an infinitely tender God, who loves each of us beyond our wildest imaginings. We can't earn that, and nothing can change it. And each of our brothers and sisters shares this great gift too!

Oratio

Jesus, help me to enter more deeply into relationship with you. Teach me to hear your voice each moment of my life, and to see every person as a reflection of your love. It can be hard to realize that even those who have hurt me or caused me pain are also your children, created in your image. Teach me to understand the truth that each person is infinitely loved and precious, yet also deeply limited and poor. With Saint Paul, I place my trust in you, remembering that ". . . we hold this treasure in earthen vessels . . ." (2 Cor 4:7).

Contemplatio

Jesus, I desire to worship you in spirit and in truth.

Wednesday of the Fifth Week
of Ordinary Time

❖‥‥‥‥‥❖

Lectio

Mark 7:14–23

Meditatio

". . . from his heart. . . ."

Today's brief Gospel reading continues the discussion about ritual purity. Jesus' contemporaries highly valued external practices of purification, especially concerning clean and unclean foods.

After the discussion, when Jesus is at home, he educates his disciples by further explaining what he means. He proposes an earthy example that they can easily understand. What goes into a person is not what defiles, because it travels through the digestive system and is eliminated.

Instead, Jesus stresses, *what truly defiles is that which comes out of the human heart*. This point is so vital that the Gospel writer repeats it within the space of a few verses.

A list of sins and vices is given, showing the various ways that our hearts can bring forth evil. Opposed to these are the virtues, which represent the kind of moral purification pleasing to God. The fruit of love for God and for others is of greater value than showy, external deeds.

The sins listed in this passage start with "evil thoughts," and continue with vices that are bred in the mind. This seems to indicate that our thoughts control the desires of our hearts. Mental discipline can promote what is true, good, beautiful, and worthy of our human dignity.

A religious founder of the twentieth century, Blessed James Alberione, called this process "the sanctification of the mind." It consists of forming the mind in healthy ways so that it can grow naturally and spiritually. The hoped-for result is to reach what Saint Paul wrote to the Romans: ". . . be transformed by the renewal of your mind, that you may discern what is the will of God, what is good and pleasing and perfect" (12:2).

Oratio

Jesus, my Master, sanctify my mind and heart. Aware of the influence that the mind exerts on my heart, help me to be attentive to the thoughts I consider, and discerning about the amount of limitless information and entertainment I choose to take in. I desire to replace unworthy thoughts with those that are pleasing to you.

Contemplatio

Turn my mind and heart toward you, Lord.

Thursday of the Fifth Week
of Ordinary Time

⁘ · · · · · · · · · · · · ⁘

Lectio

Mark 7:24–30

Meditatio

"Let the children be fed first."

We who are used to the Good Shepherd, the gentle for-giver of sins, may find this Gospel baffling. Who among us would spurn a mother pleading for the life of her child? Yet that is what Jesus seems to do. Why would he be unmoved by her tears, only to suddenly reverse his decision after her quick answer? What's going on in this Gospel, and what does it mean for us?

Jesus is in Gentile territory. This woman hears about him and rushes to ask for a miracle for her daughter. Mark's Gospel closely links Jesus' miracles with his teaching. The miracles are a sign of the kingdom of God breaking into the world and into people's lives. Here, however, Jesus has not been teaching. This Gentile woman is looking for a cure for her daughter without reference to who Jesus is. She only knows that he works miracles, and she is taking advantage of this opportunity.

Jesus lets her know his terms: his miracles are part of a larger context of salvation history in which the children of

Israel come first. Thus, the children are fed, and it is not right to give that food to the dogs (a reference to the Gentiles).

The woman replies with an act of faith that God's power is at work in this Jewish rabbi who stands before her: you have preached to the Jews, surely there must be something left for the Gentiles. Thus, the dogs eat the children's scraps.

The woman has no claims to assistance, no right to receive his favor, but depends solely on his graciousness. With another act of faith she leaves him, trusting his word when he tells her that her daughter is well. It is only when she arrives home that she sees her daughter asleep in her bed, healed.

Like this woman, we do not deserve any miraculous interventions in our life. We depend solely on grace. This dependence must be marked by faith—a faith that places absolute trust in God's word.

Oratio

Lord, sometimes I boss you about, telling you what to do for me or others. I am sorry. Lord, increase my faith.

Contemplatio

I depend on you, Lord, for everything.

Friday of the Fifth Week
of Ordinary Time

⁝ · · · · · · · · · · · · ⁝

Lectio

Mark 7:31–37

Meditatio

"[Jesus] took him off by himself, away from the crowd . . ."

Most of us who have older members in our family or community are painfully aware of the anxiety, confusion, and frustration that the hard of hearing face each day. It can seem to them at times that the world is pushing by them without a backward glance.

Jesus offers us one more glimpse into the depths of his compassionate heart as he leads the deaf man gently to the side of the crowd, not to isolate him, but to heal him. Today's Gospel reading calls me to ponder Jesus' availability and readiness to help someone in need. The journey that Jesus and his band of followers had just completed was not a leisurely walk. Presumably the group is tired, dusty, and ready for rest and a meal, not for a healing service. Jesus' love and compassion give him the strength to be there for this man and his concerned family and friends, even though Jesus is just as tired as the others. He shows us once more that love is gilded by the touch of personal sacrifice. He even utters a special word as the first word this man would hear: "*Ephphatha*"—be opened!

Jesus' gentle reaching out did not stop with his public ministry but continues for us today. The deafness that needs to be approached with compassion is not only the physical kind. We all need help in hearing God's word. Do I perceive sometimes that the Lord is leading me aside from the busyness of everyday life to help me to be more open to his word? Am I ready to put my pet projects on hold in order to be with the Lord for a while, just to listen?

Ephphatha is a word full of meaning. Jesus speaks to us, and bids us be open to his word and to the people who make up our world—those who live in our neighborhood and all over the earth. The Good News is given to be communicated. Am I ready to do my part?

Oratio

Jesus, help me to see with your eyes, and love with your heart. I want to be part of the spread of your kingdom, but I need your help to be generous and ready. Give me the trust of the deaf man who followed you unquestioningly, trusting that you were there to help. Give me some of the strength of your compassion so I will truly be your hands and eyes and heart.

Contemplatio

"*Ephphatha!*" Be opened . . .

Saturday of the Fifth Week of Ordinary Time

⟸·············⟹

Lectio

Mark 8:1–10

Meditatio

"They ate and were satisfied."

How many times a day do I actually eat? Whether it's a meal or a snack, I eat often enough. Granted, the day is full of comings and goings, work and conversations, but it's punctuated by food now and again.

Today's Gospel centers on our need for food. The Gospel invites us to walk along with the great crowd that is following Jesus. We walk amid this gigantic mass of human beings, beneath the hot sun, and we keep our eyes glued on the Teacher. We are all hungry and thirsty for God, and somehow we see God in the words and workings of this man called Jesus. We keep hanging out here with him, and soon enough three days pass and we realize we have not eaten.

Jesus turns to his disciples and tells them how his heart is moved for the crowd. He decides to feed us this day, enlisting the assistance of his special friends, the disciples. He gives us bread and fish after he has offered the traditional thanksgiving prayer, breaking the bread into pieces and having his disciples distribute it to us. Even before this miracle unfolds, though, my heart has been burning enough to follow him and hang on his every word.

Jesus cares enough to feed me every day with the bread of God's word, the fish of God's providence. What repast is he offering me today? The times I stop to eat today can be moments when I look back in gratitude on the word of this day's Gospel. What is he providing?

He is the only one who can truly satisfy me and the desires of my heart. He wants to feed me, to nurture my life. How will I let him accomplish this today? What type of thanksgiving will I offer?

Oratio

Jesus Master, I follow you, hungry for so many things. Let me feed on your word and find the wisdom that will satisfy my heart. You nurture my life with many material goods and also with everlasting realities. Let the certainty of eternal life, and you as my ultimate end, guide my steps today. Are there people around me who are hungry, whether materially or spiritually? In thanks, I will reach out to them and feed them as you have fed me.

Contemplatio

"My heart is moved with pity for the crowd. . . ."

Sixth Sunday of Ordinary Time — Year A

⁝·············⁝

Lectio

Matthew 5:17–37

Meditatio

". . . unless your righteousness surpasses . . ."

How surprised the disciples must have been when Jesus said they had to be better than the religious professionals of their time! How did the disciples interpret that? How do we understand it today?

Little by little, the Sermon on the Mount and the entire Gospel according to Matthew clarify Jesus' meaning: refraining from evil acts isn't enough. Keeping small precepts isn't enough. The roots of evil—both thoughts and desires—have to be eradicated. Good attitudes are to be cultivated, such as poverty of spirit and cleanness of heart. Good deeds are to be done, such as feeding the hungry and visiting the sick.

Saint Matthew's Gospel makes it clear that *not doing evil* is just the beginning; there's a whole "world" of good to be done! "Don't hurt others" is only one side of the coin; "do help them" is the second side. We're asked to "go beyond."

Jesus proclaims the Beatitudes in Matthew 5:3–12. He points out some works of mercy in Matthew 25:35–36. Other works of mercy include: to instruct the uneducated, to advise the unsure, to comfort the sorrowful, to forgive those who hurt us, to challenge the wayward, to pray for the living and deceased. . . .

No one is asked to do everything. Each of us is called to find his or her own way—praying for guidance and choosing the good deeds that we know or think are the best for us to do here and now. The Gospel doesn't give us a blueprint for our lives; each of us has to be open to the Spirit. For some, it will mean more external activity, and for others, more prayer or sufferings to offer for others.

While reading *The Greatest Generation*, I was reminded of the spirit that's encouraged in Matthew's Gospel. Author Tom Brokaw often refers to the way the young people who came of age in the 1940s shouldered responsibility. The privations of the Depression years and the discipline of the war effort shaped them into creative adults. That's what Jesus calls his followers to be: responsible and creative persons, formed by sacrifice and self-discipline. Are we up to the challenge?

Oratio

Father in heaven, help me to use my freedom wisely and well. Teach me to recognize the Ten Commandments as the foundation on which to build the generous life of a true follower of Jesus Christ, your Son. Sensitize me to the action of your Spirit, who moves when and where he wills. Amen.

Contemplatio

Go beyond.

Sixth Sunday of Ordinary Time —
Year B

⁘ ············ ⁘

Lectio

Mark 1:40–45

Meditatio

"The leprosy left him immediately."

I have been praying with these few verses from Mark for a few days and have experienced some dryness. Today as I sat down to pray I reminded God of my overdue deadline and that I needed him to speak to me *now*. Then he helped me understand that he has been speaking to me all along, but I wasn't able to hear him because it wasn't the answer I expected.

Our world and our society are all about "instant" or "immediate." We grumble if the checkout line doesn't move fast enough, or if our Internet connection takes more than a couple of seconds to get us online. In fact, people often say, "I want it done yesterday." All this immediate or instant gratification of our needs and desires has allowed us to lose sight of the time some things take to naturally reach a desired effect. No matter how much fertilizer we pile on a newly planted seed, the flower will not appear in the next twenty seconds if it grows normally.

Today we read about a man who is suffering from leprosy. He makes a simple statement of faith but he attaches no time frame for when he would like his healing to take place. What Jesus does in healing him instantly goes beyond the natural and is pure, miraculous gift. In the twenty-first century we might fail to see the incredible miracle of such immediate healing, because we demand the immediate in all aspects of our lives. This desire for an immediate response is a kind of virus that can overtake our spiritual life as we demand that God act in a certain way.

What is immediate is God's outpouring of his grace and love. These gifts are abundant and constant, and they make everything else in life a bit more bearable.

Oratio

Everything in my day seems to be a rush. I run out the door in the morning and keep running until my head hits the pillow at night. Lord, I do not want my relationship with you to be the same. Help me to step away from the rushing, the running, and the desire for immediate and quick answers to all life's problems. I wish today to revel in your love for me. With your grace, help me to handle with Christ-like love everything that comes my way. Amen.

Contemplatio

Give me patience, O Lord.

Sixth Sunday of Ordinary Time —
Year C

⁝・・・・・・・・・・・⁝

Lectio

Luke 6:17, 20–26

Meditatio

"Leap for joy on that day!"

What a scene change from two Sundays ago! Jesus' boyhood neighbors had raged when he contrasted their smugness toward his prophetic mission with the Gentiles' openness. He seemed to dangle his wonder-working power in front of them and foretold that he would heal the nations in body and spirit because of their acceptance. In today's reading, people do gather from beyond Israel's borders for this teaching and healing.

According to God's criteria, these poor who believe in Jesus outshine the rich who don't, and God can do "great things" for them (Lk 1:49). Paul adds why: "God chose . . . those who count for nothing, to reduce to nothing those who are something, so that no human being might boast before God" (1 Cor 1:28–29).

How can the rich share in the blessings promised to the poor? The rest of Jesus' teaching outlines the process of ongoing conversion to God's standards. It pits trust in God's power to save against the dead end of self-reliance. With this conversion comes the kingdom of joy.

The Gospel of Luke and the Acts of the Apostles hum with this joy. Pregnant with John the Baptist, Elizabeth exclaims, ". . . the infant in my womb leaped for joy" (Lk 1:44). Jesus "rejoiced [in] the holy Spirit" because through the disciples, the Father crushed diabolic conceit and blessed the childlike (Lk 10:21). In Acts, Luke points to this same Spirit's gift of joy through the Apostles' ministry. The lame beggar, once cured, "leaped up . . . and went into the temple . . . walking and jumping and praising God" (Acts 3:8).

Jesus promised that his joy would be in us, and that on his return our joy would be complete. The condition: remaining in him through a life of faith and love (see Jn 15:1ff.).

Oratio

Jesus Master, you spoke with authority and credibility. Your teaching reflected who you are, God's Word, but it rings true with us because you lived what we all live. Help me not to fall for the false promises of the "prosperity Gospel," touted by many pseudo-evangelists as your word. Give me the real joy that comes from you regardless of my situation. Renew my hope for the fullness of joy that no one will take away from me (see Jn 16:22).

Contemplatio

"The hungry he has filled with good things; the rich he has sent away empty" (Lk 1:53).

Monday of the Sixth Week
of Ordinary Time

∴ · · · · · · · · · · · · ∴

Lectio

Mark 8:11–13

Meditatio

"Amen, I say to you, no sign will be given to this generation."

The Pharisees ask for a sign, but Jesus refuses to grant their request. Why doesn't he fulfill it? He fulfills other requests for healing. Aren't those requests granting a sign to the person asking? So what's the difference? In the Gospel accounts, when Jesus grants someone's request to be healed, he generally links this with the faith of the person requesting the healing. Could it be that the Pharisees are lacking faith?

In many ways, we can be like the Pharisees in our relationship with God. We may ask God to grant us signs—not because we believe, but in order to satisfy ourselves and our needs. If the sign itself is not to our satisfaction, we often don't recognize it. We may even reject it.

This indicates that our relationship with God is not based on a mature faith. Rather, it is based on an immature faith, faith that can be manipulative. As long as my relationship with God remains on this level, I am actually deciding for myself, according to my likes and dislikes, who God is. I am not sincerely seeking God as he is. In a way, I am putting God to the test—judging him. And if he doesn't measure up to my expectations? Forget it.

God will not be manipulated. He will not be a puppet performing tricks on demand. God's signs are discerned by those whose eyes and ears are open. They need no signs because they are able to perceive God's loving presence through all of his creative works. To them God is truly revealed, for they allow God's work to speak to them of God and they begin to know him as he is. They do not impose their own reality onto God, onto themselves, onto others, or onto what God has created. They allow reality, including the reality of who God truly is, to be revealed to them.

Oratio

Jesus, I seek security. When I lose my sense of security, I make demands of you. Like a child testing a relationship, I test you. I often do not believe that you are taking care of me. And when I don't get what I ask you for, that belief is reinforced. It's like I'm playing a game with you. How many signs of your care have I missed because I have already decided what I need and haven't gotten it? I need to let go of my childishness. Help me to become mature in my faith. Amen.

Contemplatio

Lord, you feed the birds of the sky. Yet we are far more important to you than they (see Mt 6:26).

Tuesday of the Sixth Week
of Ordinary Time

✦ · · · · · · · · · · · · ✦

Lectio

Mark 8:14–21

Meditatio

"Do you still not understand?"

Some years ago I worked with someone who came from another country. We spoke the same language—or so we thought—but some misunderstandings would invariably arise. She would explain something, and I would understand it according to my cultural lens and life experience. Later, I would find out that what I heard was not what she intended to communicate. There was more to the message than I could take in. It seems to be our human condition to live with the imperfection of communication.

In this passage from Mark, Jesus expresses his frustration: "do you still not understand?" Before this, he tries to help the disciples recall—"Do you have eyes and not see, ears and not hear? And do you not remember, when I broke the five loaves for the five thousand . . . ?"

Jesus' frustration here is more than the human struggle of miscommunication due to language. As we have been reading in Mark, Jesus has performed miracles, called for faith, and manifested the coming of the kingdom. But the disciples simply cannot take it all in. They are blind and deaf as far as recognizing the true significance of Jesus' words, actions, and presence.

As I pray over this passage, Jesus' words to the disciples do not sound harsh. I hear the sadness of Jesus as he longs for the disciples to fully understand what is taking place before their very eyes. I can hear him ask me, as he asks the disciples, "do you still not understand?" Daily I witness so many blessings that manifest Jesus as my Savior and Lord, yet how often am I blinded by my own preoccupation, nearsightedness, lack of gratitude? Jesus calls me—and each one of us—by name, as he questions, "Will you open the eyes of your heart and believe in me?"

Oratio

Jesus, increase my faith in you as my Savior and Lord. As you daily manifest your saving love in little and big ways, open my eyes to recognize your grace. Thank you for your patience with me when I am slow to understand. Help me to see you more clearly, to listen more profoundly as I approach the Sacred Scripture and the Eucharist. In the daily effort of communicating with my brothers and sisters, may I hear your voice and speak your words. May I recognize you in all things.

Contemplatio

Open my eyes to recognize you, my Lord, in all things.

Wednesday of the Sixth Week of Ordinary Time

∴ ⋯⋯⋯⋯ ∴

Lectio

Mark 8:22–26

Meditatio

"People brought to him a blind man and begged Jesus to touch him."

Jesus is on the road to Bethsaida, and he has just finished correcting his disciples for their slowness in understanding what he is about. Then Jesus spies a small group of people waiting for him at the village gates with a blind man. They beg Jesus to touch this man. They have understood, as perhaps none of the disciples yet has, that Jesus waits for us to ask, to present our need and express our trust. Jesus leads the man outside the village and cures him in a gradual way, questioning him and touching him again until he is able to "see everything distinctly."

Soon this man will be shocked into the daylight and the hurly-burly of life in a fishing village. Jesus' tact and kindness are so clear, and his care for this man is so divine, yet so human. Jesus sends him home, telling him not even to go into the village, for he has just looked into the eyes of his Savior.

There is a deeper lesson here than meets the eye. In my heart of hearts, I want to be the blind man whom Jesus treats so gently. And I am. But I also feel like his disciples, who are still smarting from Jesus' exasperation. I, too, can't wrap my mind around the whole picture of this kingdom that Jesus speaks of. I sense a strange mix of faith, doubt, love, and frustration simmering in my soul.

The honesty to acknowledge these feelings comes from the Lord. They show that I have entered into this moment, and that I am ready to embrace Jesus' Good News as my own, even though I know not precisely how. Like the blind man, I will need to stand ready for Jesus' healing touch until I can see clearly. I am sure of one thing: Jesus will never say, "No more. I have no more healing touch for you."

Oratio

Good Jesus, you left us so many precious proofs of your personal love and interest in the lives of the people you met and lived with. I wonder how you would like living in this day and age . . . . But you *do*, don't you? You count my every sigh and dry my every teardrop; you stand by me when I feel weak and afraid. Help me remember more often that there is nothing you cannot do for me if I trust. And I ask you to help me overcome my lack of trust, so that I will not keep you waiting . . . .

Contemplatio

Find your peace in trust.

Thursday of the Sixth Week
of Ordinary Time

∴ ⋯⋯⋯⋯ ∴

Lectio

Mark 8:27–33

Meditatio

> *". . . the Son of Man must suffer greatly . . ."*

In today's Gospel, Jesus asks his disciples, "Who do people say that I am?" And then, "But who do *you* say that I am?"

When we hear Peter answer for the disciples that Jesus is "the Christ," that sounds like the end of the story. But Jesus, in effect, tells them that they've only gotten halfway. "The Son of Man must suffer greatly. . . ."

In some ways, you could envision this scene in terms of people in a special relationship. As things progress, one or the other may say something like, "Before we go any further, there's something you need to know. . . ." It's the opening to a deeper revelation about the person, but a truth that could complicate things. If that revelation is accepted, this moment becomes a turning point in the relationship. From then on, the story that was revealed will be a shared story, a place of intimate communion.

Today people are rather free in giving their opinions about who Jesus is. Ancient holy man. Jewish peasant who didn't mean for any of this history-changing stuff to happen. Prophet. Myth. Bodhisattva. Even "highly evolved consciousness" (really!). It's just as challenging now as it was two thousand years ago to accept the folly of the cross (see I Cor 1:18), and to accept what being "the Christ" really means. That's because (as Peter intuited when he tried to talk that folly out of Jesus) it means accepting our own share in the sufferings of Christ and the glory to be revealed (see I Pt 4:13).

Oratio

Lord Jesus, my immediate reaction to your revelation tends to be just like Peter's. Thinking on the purely practical level, I cannot see how suffering and rejection could be part of the picture of salvation. But when suffering does come into my life, it is so consoling to realize that you know from the inside what it is like. For a little while, you were "made lower than the angels. . . . For it was fitting that he, for whom and through whom all things exist, in bringing many children to glory, should make the leader to their salvation perfect through suffering" (Heb 2:9–10).

Contemplatio

He has borne our griefs and carried our sorrows (see Is 53:4–5).

Friday of the Sixth Week
of Ordinary Time

⁝∙∙∙∙∙∙∙∙∙∙∙∙⁝

Lectio

Mark 8:34–9:1

Meditatio

> *"What profit is there for one*
> *to gain the whole world and forfeit his life?"*

It's said that Francis Xavier, a student who expected to pursue a brilliant secular career, was thoroughly annoyed whenever an older colleague, Ignatius of Loyola, asked the question above. We know that eventually Ignatius won the battle of wills. Francis gave up his promising career to become a priest and one of the most-traveled missionary saints.

The word rendered as "life" in today's Gospel passage can mean both "life" and "soul." Ignatius had warned the younger man that he was planning to embark on a dangerous course. It was difficult to remain a man of principle while pursuing fame and fortune. Francis' soul might have been at risk.

The thrust of today's Gospel passage is self-denial and carrying the cross. Self-denial and sacrifice, Jesus tells his disciples, are the means for keeping one's life/soul safe. Exegetes tell us that "denying" means disowning. One who practices self-denial ceases to regard self as the center of the universe. Instead, this person becomes focused on God and others.

Surely Xavier became other-centered as he traveled through India, the Molucca Islands, and other lands of the Far East, proclaiming the Good News, receiving thousands into the Church and catechizing his new Christians by means of stories and songs.

Probably none of us will ever become another Xavier, but if we look around we may find ways we can bring people closer to God. And if we don't see how, we can ask the Lord for guidance, because he knows what he'd like us to do. This, then, is a way we can deny ourselves.

But where does the cross come in?

We don't have to look for the cross. *It* will find *us*.

Oratio

Jesus, Divine Master, help me to recognize that my life shouldn't revolve around me. Although I do have to take care of my health, livelihood, and appearance, you created me to also reach out to help others. I may not be another Xavier, but under your guidance I want to share the Christian message with my family, friends, and colleagues. Inspire me to use for others the talents you have given me. Let me step back and take the third place, preceded by you and the people you want me to help.

Contemplatio

I want the third place.

Saturday of the Sixth Week
of Ordinary Time

⋮⋅⋅⋅⋅⋅⋅⋅⋅⋅⋅⋅⋅⋮

Lectio

Mark 9:2–13

Meditatio

> *". . . and he was transfigured before them . . . ."*

The Gospel doesn't say that Jesus was "transformed." He
didn't undergo an actual change of substance, only a change
of outer appearance. The shining white of his clothes (and,
in the story as told by Matthew and Luke, also of his face)
is a glimpse of the glory that Jesus already had as eternal Son
of the Father, but which was hidden from the eyes of those
who lived with him. During his earthly life, his glory was not
physically evident, but on this occasion, the chosen three get
a special glimpse into his deeper reality.

This Gospel story reminds me of the concept of a parallel universe, sometimes used in science fiction and fantasy
writing. In this idea, someone finds a point of contact or a
portal between two separate "realities." In the transfiguration
of Jesus, it's as if a parallel universe of eternity is briefly
perceived in time. On that mountaintop there is a connection
with the eternal world, which we will one day enter, where the
Son of God dwells in glory.

Perhaps it would be good to imagine the parallel universe that is linked to our lives, too. What is the deeper reality behind the ordinary people in our lives? If we could see them as God does—from the other side of eternity—what would they look like? There might be dazzlingly beautiful people all around us! If we could see the hidden acts of charity that many people carry out, the joy with which they give of themselves, the love with which they carry their crosses, we might be blinded by the spectacle. But God doesn't allow us to see this deeper truth during our lifetime. We have to wait until we pass to eternity through the portal of death. Then we will be transformed and able to see the truth that is hidden from us in life.

Oratio

Jesus, help me remember that you see things differently than we human beings do. You see the deeper reality of the heart, which is hidden from us. When I am discouraged by my efforts that seem to come to nothing, remind me of my own hidden glory. Help me recall the hidden beauty and glory that may be concealed in the people around me—those closest to me and the strangers I come in contact with.

Contemplatio

God sees beyond our appearance and into our hearts.

Seventh Sunday of Ordinary Time —
Year A

∴ · · · · · · · · · · · ∴

Lectio

Matthew 5:38–48

Meditatio

". . . love your enemies . . ."

Three words—three words that intimately affect every one of us. It took me more than fifteen years of struggle to forgive someone who had had a major negative impact on my teenage years. Often I thought I had forgiven and found closure, but then the pain would reappear unexpectedly. Whether individually or as a family, or church, or country, we often face the monumental task of integrating an experience of evil into our lives in a precisely *Christian* manner. We can't escape this difficult experience. Sometimes it seems impossible. It often takes a long time.

The three words, "love your enemies" are the key to facing evil and injustice. Jesus is not speaking of a sentimental kind of love. He is not asking us to condone injustice or victimization. He is not asking us to let others off the hook. He is not suggesting we tolerate them or, heaven forbid, allow them to continue to harm us or another. Instead, this call to love our enemies is a call to want the best for the other person. Jesus explains it by commanding us to "do good to those who hate you, bless those who curse you, pray for those who mistreat you" (Lk 6:27–28).

Such love is a choice, an act of the will, which we can make despite the natural repugnance we may feel for what the other has done. It is a choice to be positive to that person. To practice this love, which Jesus showed us on the cross, is difficult. The first step is to pray for the healing of painful memories, to invite Jesus directly into the experience of evil. If the hurt is severe, we may need to pray for the miracle of forgiveness. We may need counseling to free us from acting out of past negative experiences. Jesus asks us to break the spiral of violence and hatred by not passing it on, by wishing well instead of ill, by being willing to offer our lives for our brothers and sisters.

Oratio

Jesus, you show me that love is the only way to achieve anything. Every page of the Gospel shows me that this is true. Even though you were God, you didn't act as if you were entitled to special treatment or put yourself above the sufferings and injustices that we experience at the hands of others. What made you different is that you didn't strike back. Jesus, give me a big heart; help me to really care about others, even if I suffer at their hands. And when I need a miracle to help me forgive, please grant me this grace. Amen.

Contemplatio

Thank you, my Jesus, for forgiving me.

Seventh Sunday of Ordinary Time — Year B

∴ · · · · · · · · · · · ∴

Lectio

Mark 2:1–12

Meditatio

> *"After they had broken through. . . ."*

As you read this account of the paralytic's cure, have you ever wondered whether the four men were friends, or simply friends of a friend, doing a favor? Does it really matter? The important fact for us is that these four men are teaching a lesson on prayer, on connection with the Lord. The people of Capernaum are excited because Jesus is home. Fortunately for us, Jesus is always at home, even if it doesn't always seem that way when we pray. But in this story, most of the town is gathered at the house where Jesus is teaching. They crowd in, blocking the doors and windows. The four men arrive late, probably because of the effort to bring their paralyzed friend. Once there, they can't get in. Undeterred, they struggle up to the roof. The house isn't large, so they can tell by the sound of his voice exactly where Jesus is. They gently set the paralyzed man down and start to pull off the roofing. Then they lower the paralytic through the hole they have made.

We try to picture this. They probably don't have rope, but they have their own cloaks. Perhaps they tie them two by two and tuck them under the man's mat. Taking the corners in hand they lower him into the outstretched arms of Jesus' listeners.

"After they had broken through": we need to hear these words. We may often feel we can't get near to Jesus, so we stand apart with our needs. We feel some kind of block. The four men show us the way: carry the burden, climb to the roof, remove the obstacle, improvise a way to lower the problem before Jesus.

Without a word, Jesus forgives the man, and immediately the buzz of indignation begins. So Jesus asks the crowd which is easier to do: forgive or cure? We should expect both. This is the second lesson on prayer for us. Our sins will be forgiven, *and* our negative outlook, our disappointment, our depression will be cured if we act in faith.

Oratio

Give us the faith of these four men so that all the corners of our doubt and all of our questioning will be brought before you. We want to believe. We want to pray. Free us from our paralysis. Strengthen us and encourage our daily effort. Jesus, Physician and Friend, grant us holy initiative and confidence in your loving care.

Contemplatio

Your faith has saved you.

Seventh Sunday of Ordinary Time— Year C

∴ · · · · · · · · · · · · ∴

Lectio

Luke 6:27–38

Meditatio

"Be merciful, just as your Father is merciful."

Jesus had already lived in the tiny village of Nazareth for thirty years before he uttered these words. He had been the compassionate witness of our human need for love, and our all too human reluctance to overlook, to let things go. Jesus had seen our unwillingness to cover with love the slights and injustices that pepper our days. With his family and neighbors he had faced life under the shadow of the occupying Roman forces. Jesus had witnessed his people's longing for the Messiah, for a time of righteousness that seemed too distant an ideal.

The crowd now listening to Jesus' words seems to be a silent crowd. We know it is a big crowd, for this is part of Jesus' important discourse on discipleship. Luke situates it on the Plain, while Matthew places the famous Sermon on the Mount on a higher area. Jesus' words, which define so plainly our way of discipleship, reveal how much courage Jesus is asking from those who would be his true followers.

When Jesus asks us to forgive, to do unto others what we would want done to ourselves, he is asking us to move to a higher level of relationship—one that will allow us to live as members of the family of God, who is kind and forgiving even to those without gratitude and without love. But the reward Jesus holds out to us *is* great, worth any effort we make to try to see others through the loving gaze of God. "Forgive and you will be forgiven. Give, and gifts will be given to you; a good measure, packed together, shaken down, and overflowing, will be poured into your lap."

Oratio

Good Jesus, only you could have asked this kind of love from us—you who loved us to the end. When I am caught up in the petty dramas of everyday life, your plea for a loving, forgiving heart falls far from my attention, and often I fail. Teach me that if I love myself because I am sure of your love, it will be easier for me. Then I will be able to take a moment and arm myself with mercy as I reel from a thoughtless word or an unkind deed, to intercept the offense and diffuse it with love—*your* love, the Father's love.

Contemplatio

"You will be children of the Most High."

Monday of the Seventh Week of Ordinary Time

∴ · · · · · · · · · · · · ∴

Lectio

Mark 9:14–29

Meditatio

"I do believe, help my unbelief!"

Here in today's Gospel passage is a man who has tried everything to bring healing to his son, but to no avail. Not even the disciples of Jesus, who up to now had been able to cast out demons, are able to help him. This man's hopes have been dwindling for years. But his love for his son gives him the courage to try again when he sees the Master approaching.

". . . *If* you can do anything, have compassion on us and help us." This is no longer the clear light of a simple faith. This is a man who has journeyed through dark and difficult years. He has experienced doubt and fear. So many failed efforts have dulled his faith, perhaps leaving him with many questions: "Where is God? Why is he allowing this?" Perhaps he is even afraid to hope, lest he be disappointed again. Into this place of darkness, Jesus brings a challenge and an invitation: "'If you can!' Everything is possible to one who has faith!"

And with that invitation, something awakens in the very depths of this father's heart. A cry emerges—a reawakening of hope. He recognizes his own weakness, his own need of the Lord's assistance to help him make this leap of faith. "I do believe, help my unbelief!"

How often I have felt my own heart echoing the cry of this father on behalf of his son! I, too, struggle to believe during moments of darkness, when God's plan is cast in shadow and uncertainty. Like this father, we, too, have family members who struggle with illness or pain. We, too, know what it is to deeply desire change or healing, and to feel as though God is silent. These moments challenge and invite us to go beyond our childhood faith into an adult faith that embraces the mystery of the cross. Are we ready to receive the invitation?

Oratio

Lord, gift me with a faith that is strong and deep, one that can weather the storms of life. You never promised that my walk with you would be easy. Instead, you promised that we need not be afraid, because no matter what challenges or sufferings we face, you will always be with us. Help me to believe this, and to place myself and my loved ones continually into your loving hands. I do not always understand your ways, but I know and believe that you desire my good, and the good of all. Root me and ground me in your love, and help me to *believe* you are present and at work.

Contemplatio

Jesus, increase my faith!

Tuesday of the Seventh Week
of Ordinary Time

⁘ · · · · · · · · · · · ⁘

Lectio

Mark 9:30–37

Meditatio

". . . the greatest . . ."

Did you ever hear toddlers squabble over the same toy?
They're only a little less sophisticated than the disciples in
today's Gospel, who jockey for a position in the kingdom—a
kingdom, Jesus points out, that's run (or overrun) by kids!

Jesus Christ is no Peter Pan, marketing a world where the
young never grow up. No, Jesus says, the kingdom is not that
kind of world. Its members are not that kind of kid—they're
this kind, and he tenderly draws into their circle a trusting,
unpretentious child, a parable in person. This scene immediately follows Jesus' prediction of the Passion. So that child
becomes a symbol of Jesus himself, embracing his death and
placing his future into the Father's saving, re-creative hands.

This child of God also symbolizes us, who claim to be
his, who trust the Father so much that we lay down our lives
for one another, confident that God will "raise us also with
Jesus" (2 Cor 4:14). These are the servants Jesus models, not
those who just do good things for others—that's philanthro-
py—but who courageously do whatever it takes to live and

die for others' good. That's love. They're the foot-washing, Eucharistic kind, who in their paschal rebirth mirror the One who nourishes others so they can live.

Human limitations aside, it takes both childlike openness and maturing faith to imagine how God can and does choose "those who count for nothing," as Paul observes, and leads them to this greatness, that rests "not on human wisdom but on the power of God" (1 Cor 1:28, 2:5).

Faith-filled openness requires vulnerability. But that's the last thing we want. We'll connive, sweat, battle it out. We'll go down in flames before we're caught without our guns. So we compensate with this or that, until we discover to our dismay that none of it has protected us from life after all. Painful as it can be, it's also liberating to surrender to love. "For freedom Christ set us free . . ." (Gal 5:1).

Oratio

Lord, help me to resurrender every day, but to focus only on today. I cringe at having to form new attitudes and to learn new skills, but learning is a child's fascinating, wonder-filled adventure, especially if you're the Teacher. I open my arms to everything and everyone you have for me, sure that beyond the sometimes crucifying pain this openness brings, new life awaits me and those you give me to love.

Contemplatio

I want to free someone else today through my self-sacrifice to love.

Wednesday of the Seventh Week
of Ordinary Time

:·············:

Lectio

Mark 9:38–40

Meditatio

"Do not prevent him."

Can we picture John being brought up short by this response from Jesus? In John's mind, undoubtedly, he and his companions are Jesus' chosen ones—the Master's special inner circle. How can this other fellow, who has no connection with them, *presume* to cast out demons in Jesus' name? It just isn't right. . . .

But here is Jesus calmly saying, "Whoever is not against us is for us." Does John swallow an unspoken "But . . ."?

Haven't we all been in similar situations? *We* were the insiders, the rising stars, the generous staff members who worked day and night for the success of our organization. Whenever an "upstart" appeared, he or she was cordially resented.

Think back to some such situation in your life. . . . How did it work out? Did you learn anything from the way things developed? Would you have handled matters differently if you could live through that experience again?

I think each of us can admit that what we just recalled was a moment of jealousy and fear. We felt threatened. Perhaps we feared losing our job. Or perhaps something deeper disturbed us. We may have felt insecure at the very core of our being. What does one *do* about that? How does one acquire a true sense of self-worth?

Counselors tell us it's helpful to recognize that we mean a lot to certain people. These others see something in us that we may not see in ourselves. When we feel loved by others, we can begin to recognize that *God* loves us too—with all our shortcomings. When we truly believe in God's unconditional love, we feel secure, and the presumed threats disappear.

If we haven't reached that point, it's a wonderful grace to ask for.

Oratio

Lord Jesus, Saint Paul reminds me that when I was a sinner you died for me. You love me so much, but I love myself so little! Help me to comprehend the depths of your love for all your handiwork. Teach me to love myself and to love my friends, family, and colleagues as fellow pilgrims on the way to our eternal homeland. Help me return your love by living as your true disciple. Amen.

Contemplatio

To God, each of us is special.

Thursday of the Seventh Week
of Ordinary Time

∴ · · · · · · · · · · · ∴

Lectio

Mark 9:41–50

Meditatio

"Keep salt in yourselves and you will have peace with one another."

Jesus makes clear our immense responsibility for each other, reversing the effects of that ancient question: "Am I my brother's keeper?" (Gn 4:9). God heard the blood of the slain Abel crying out from the ground and asked Cain where Abel, his brother, was. Apparently God intended us to feel responsible for each other. In his sullen response, Cain rejected any responsibility: "I don't know where he is. Am I my brother's keeper. . . ?"

Jesus reverses the attitude that had dominated the human heart from almost the dawn of creation and traces our responsibility for one another in large letters: we are responsible for others' physical well-being (". . . a cup of water to drink") and for their eternal salvation ("Whoever causes one of these little ones who believe in me to sin . . .").

In our culture we don't want to get too involved. We tolerate a lot. We keep to ourselves. If someone isn't breaking the law or bothering us, we don't concern ourselves with what that person is doing, but that's not the Christian way. If we are worth our salt, if we are the salt of the earth and our salt has not gone insipid, then we will care about another's eternal salvation. If anything about our lifestyle or behavior causes another to sin, then we must "pluck it out" lest we be thrown into Gehenna. We cannot control others, but we can keep salt in ourselves through prayer, personal growth in discipleship, and an ever deeper understanding of Jesus' message and the Church's teaching. By seeking the good of others, praying for them, having respectful conversations, listening to their stories, and at times even lovingly confronting them, we fulfill our responsibility as our "brother's keeper."

Oratio

These things, Father, are hard to do. They may lead to interactions that I fear will become angry and antagonistic, for nobody wants to be told what to do. But your Son Jesus said that we will have peace if we kept salt in ourselves. By "salted living" I could compassionately influence another's life for the good. Remind me that I don't have to take on the whole world, only the one or two people you send my way. Help me to care about others' physical and spiritual well-being, and to take my responsibility for good example and formative influence on others seriously.

Contemplatio

Let me recognize the people you send my way, that I may care for them as you care for me.

Friday of the Seventh Week
of Ordinary Time

⁝··············⁝

Lectio

Mark 10:1–12

Meditatio

". . . the disciples again questioned [Jesus]. . . ."

In this Gospel passage on marriage and divorce, Jesus is nothing if not direct and even blunt with the Pharisees. The Church today remains clear on where it stands on marriage and other issues.

The disciples hear the exchange between Jesus and the Pharisees and are left with some questions. According to Mosaic Law a man could divorce his wife. How could Jesus say that this was not God's original intent? The disciples are confused, so they question Jesus. Unlike the Pharisees, the disciples desire to understand better, not to trap Jesus. He does not ask them, "Is everything clear?" Instead, the disciples take the initiative to ask for clarification.

We have a similar responsibility. There are aspects of our faith that we may find difficult to accept or to completely understand. Perhaps it has to do with some of the "touchy" areas such as contraception or marriage, or even areas of doctrine, such as the real presence. None of us, regardless of age or profession, has finished learning about our faith, and we have to take the initiative to continue learning. To participate in ongoing faith formation is to follow in the footsteps of the disciples who were unafraid to admit that they did not understand Jesus' difficult teaching. We have a choice—we can choose whether or not to live in ignorance and to blindly accept or reject these aspects of our faith.

To seek faith formation is to be responsible and active in our faith and in our relationship with God, who wishes us to understand. In his first letter to the Corinthians, Saint Paul tells us that when we were children we talked and thought as children do (see 1 Cor 13:11). As adults we are called to be mature not just in age but in our faith. In asking questions about our faith we gain deeper love and insight; the only thing we lose is childish ignorance.

Oratio

Lord, I do wish to know you better by knowing my faith better. Give me the courage and the opportunity to ask you my questions and the grace of an open mind to receive your answers. Help me, Jesus, to know how you invite me today to seek this understanding. I don't know where to begin, but I trust that you do and will tell me. Lord, you wish to answer my questions and feed my hunger for knowledge—thank you. Amen.

Contemplatio

Teach me your ways, O Lord.

Saturday of the Seventh Week
of Ordinary Time

∴∴∴∴∴∴

Lectio

Mark 10:13–16

Meditatio

> ". . . accept the kingdom of God like a child. . . ."

When visiting with her grandchildren, a woman brought out a plate of fruit for them and said to her three-year-old granddaughter, "I thought you would like the strawberries, Cecilia." The little girl responded, "Nana, I like everything you give me."

Jesus must have had a child like this in mind when he said we should accept the kingdom of God as a child. But what does this mean? What is the kingdom of God, and in what way are we to accept it?

The Greek word here translated as "accept" can also be translated as "receive" or "welcome." We need not only to be open to the kingdom of God (and not reject it), but also to *welcome* it as a gift, as something that is for our benefit but is not ours by right. The theologically rich term "Kingdom of God" is used often in the Gospel of Mark, with some slightly different meanings. Basically, the kingdom of God is God's rule and authority over us. It sometimes refers to the here and now rule of God, and sometimes to the future rule of God that will only be complete in eternity.

Little Cecilia could say what she did because she knew her grandmother loved her, always gave her good things, and always intended her good. That is so much more true of God in relation to us! God loves us more than any parent or grandparent could ever love a child, more than any man or woman could love a spouse. God's love is stronger than any bond of brotherhood or sisterhood. And God's love has more power than any human love to actually bring about the good he desires.

So, whatever God wills or allows to happen will ultimately be for our good. Yet how many of us trust that love completely, unconditionally? How many of us can say, with open hearts, "Father, I like everything you give me."

Oratio

Jesus, I believe in your love for me. I know there is no reason to fear anything that may come because you love me. And even if you allow bad things to happen, with your power you can make good come out of evil. Teach me to come to you, and to the Father, with the heart of a child—not grasping or grudging, not guarded or wary, not hesitant or fearful, but open and trusting in your love.

Contemplatio

I like everything you give me, Lord.

Eighth Sunday of Ordinary Time — Year A

❖ · · · · · · · · · · · ❖

Lectio

Matthew 6:24–34

Meditatio

"Is not life more than food and the body more than clothing?"

The Lord offers his word to me. I want to take it wherever I go and allow it to speak to me. To hear it best, sometimes I need to enter the scene of the Gospel. Today I ask the word to come along as I stop a while in an area that is familiar to me: the corner of Broadway and West 38th Street in New York City.

From this vantage point, in the fashion district of one of the world's largest cities, I can look north to Times Square or south to see a large department store. In this area there is a "fashion walk" where bronze stars in the sidewalk honor many designers and their signature pieces. Here I am often struck by a message that is the exact opposite of the Gospel: clothing is all there is.

Walking with the word, I continue to my destination: Pauline Books & Media on West 38th Street between 5th and 6th avenues. This is a small and humble space, with simple wood floors and simply dressed people who offer the word of life to all who come. In this space we offer an alternative to the glitz that can sometimes entangle us. In this space, we offer a word of certainty about how God does provide for us, clothing us in unimaginable ways. In this space, we witness to the Father who knows all that we need. I'm grateful for my experience in working here, offering what seems like a small drop that can refresh and give meaning to weary lives in the grand ocean of worldly cares.

Today, wherever you go, be attentive and grateful for the ways you can offer God to the world, through your words, actions, care, optimism and hope, almsgiving, work well done. . . . Life has so much more to offer than what we worry about. In your own daily trek, the Lord will show you how to witness to the "more."

Oratio

Jesus, I'm grateful that today I am just a little more aware of your presence in my daily life. You are that "more" for which I thirst. Your life and the way you lived it are the measure for how I want to live my life. True, I don't walk the roads of Galilee or Nazareth, but I'm here and you're here. Teach me to trust in how much the Father knows me and cares for me. Teach me to see how very much more my life is because of you. Thank you for all you will show me as we go through our day together.

Contemplatio

The Father will lovingly provide . . . I make him first in my life.

Eighth Sunday of Ordinary Time — Year B

∴ · · · · · · · · · · · · ∴

Lectio

Mark 2:18–22

Meditatio

> " . . . new wine is poured into fresh wineskins."

This Gospel selection contains a lot of newness. First, Jesus refers to himself as the bridegroom. That might not seem new to us, since we have read this Gospel so many times, but it was new for the people to whom he was speaking. Throughout the Old Testament, the image of the bridegroom was often used to stand for God, but not for a prophet or even for the Messiah. For Jesus to take this divine image and apply it to himself is a surprising and new thing.

Then Jesus goes on to talk about new and old cloth, wine, and wineskins. The line from Isaiah comes to mind: "See, I am doing something new! Now it springs forth, do you not perceive it?" (Is 43:19). Jesus is trying to impress on us the newness of what he brings. His teaching, his revelation of the Father and the Spirit, and his gift of salvation mark a completely new time in history. This means that we must change as well—new knowledge of God means new ways of living and acting. Pouring this new wine into old wineskins just won't work.

But Jesus isn't saying this only about what was new at the time of his coming. This newness is something he brings into our lives every day. Each new gift, each new insight, brings the invitation to move into a new place.

For example, perhaps I have received an insight into how God's love has worked in my life through a particular person or in a painful event. That can lead me to look for God working in other situations I may previously have tried to avoid. Or if I have the grace of seeing something sinful in my life in a new light—something that I easily excused before but now realize is harmful to myself and others and is displeasing to God—then I am being invited to work on changing this behavior. New wine needs new wineskins.

Oratio

Jesus, I don't always notice the new things you do in my life. Sometimes you work so subtly and gradually that I don't notice my growth in understanding or trust or forgiveness. I want to pay more attention from now on. When I see the new things you are doing, I want to do my part by responding in love and gratitude.

Contemplatio

What new thing is God doing in my life?

Eighth Sunday of Ordinary Time — Year C

⁝ · · · · · · · · · · · · ⁝

Lectio

Luke 6:39–45

Meditatio

> *". . . from the fullness of the heart the mouth speaks."*

What fills my heart today?

During a recent retreat, the retreat director spoke of a related Gospel passage: "where your treasure is, there also will your heart be" (Mt 6:21). This reminded me that we will know what our true treasure is by looking at what occupies our thoughts, fills our desires, becomes the source of our actions and conversations. I have often read this passage in the Scriptures and automatically assumed, "Of course— Jesus is my treasure!" But this retreat reflection gave me pause. Where had my thoughts been in the past week? And if Jesus is truly my treasure, why wasn't I spending more time thinking and dreaming of him and of my desire to serve and know him better? As I looked over my recent preoccupations, I came to realize that I had been allowing other "treasures" to take up residence in my heart and mind. Other concerns, relationships, frustrations, and worries were pushing me away from my desired relationship and focus on God.

The wisdom that Jesus is imparting in today's reading is much the same. Jesus is asking us to reexamine what fills our hearts and minds. And the proof is in the fruit. What fills our conversations with family, friends, and coworkers? Are we bringing ourselves and others closer to the kingdom and thus bringing life? Or are we speaking in a way that breaks down the kingdom, perhaps even through gossip or callous jokes or words? As Jesus reminds us, "every tree is known by its own fruit." Yet Jesus is also the patient and merciful Lord of the vineyard—if we have not borne good fruit today, he continues to urge and encourage us on to bear new, more wholesome fruit tomorrow.

Oratio

Jesus, today I feel you inviting me to look more closely at what fills my mind and heart. Help me to see the ways you have enabled me to bear good fruit in my interactions so that I can give you glory. Give me the courage to face the ways that I may have lost my focus on you and on your kingdom, perhaps even bringing others with me. I ask you to help me renew my desire to have you be my one true treasure—the one who fills my mind and my heart with a store of goodness, so that I can bear good fruit in you.

Contemplatio

Jesus, help me keep my gaze fixed on you!

Monday of the Eighth Week of Ordinary Time

Lectio

Mark 10:17–27

Meditatio

"Jesus, looking at him, loved him and said. . . ."

I don't think Jesus liked flattery. When the rich man runs up, falls to his knees, and hails Jesus as "Good Teacher," the Master objects at once. Their dialogue doesn't have a happy beginning. But Jesus does reply to the man's question. He summarizes some of the commandments, including deference to parents—which suggests that the man is young.

Jesus' questioner replies eagerly that he has kept all the commandments since early adolescence.

Now the dialogue reaches its high point. Jesus looks at the rich young man with love and invites him to take the further step of selling his property and becoming an itinerant disciple. The man's face falls, and he leaves in sadness.

What had he expected? Perhaps he had wanted to be a disciple part time, without having to sell his possessions and give away the proceeds. It seems that the rich young man wanted the best of two worlds.

This makes me reflect: how important it is to pray for the men and women whom God is calling! So many other appeals come at them from all sides! Even if we don't know anyone by name, we can pray for all those unknown vocations, that "the world, the flesh, and the devil" won't lure those men and women elsewhere.

It has been pointed out that one of the best ways to foster religious vocations is to live one's own vocation well. May all of us—religious, priests, married couples, and single lay-people—live our own state in life well and enthusiastically! Let's do so while praying that the Lord may shower many graces on the young (and not-so-young) people whom he is calling to the priesthood and religious life.

Oratio

Jesus, Divine Master, our world is filled with much more noise than the bleating of horns, the babble of voices, the blaring of music, and the cacophony of ring tones. There are siren songs that may smother your still, small voice speaking to the hearts of men and women whom you wish to follow you more closely. How can they hear you in the midst of all this din? Please break through their "deafness," as you did with Saint Augustine. I offer you my resolution to live my own vocation with dedication and joy. Please accept my life as a continuous prayer for the men and women you want to follow you in the ordained and consecrated life.

Contemplatio

Live life well!

Tuesday of the Eighth Week
of Ordinary Time

⁑ · · · · · · · · · · · ⁑

Lectio

Mark 10:28–31

Meditatio

> *"Peter began to say to Jesus,*
> *'We have given up everything and followed you.'"*

Peter wants to know what the consequences will be. He and the other disciples have left all they held dear to follow Jesus. They have fallen in love with Jesus, who is everything for them. They left their families, jobs, conveniences, comfort, and security—everything—for the sake of Jesus. This man whom they have come to believe is the Son of Man, the Messiah, has looked on them with love and called them to be close to him—poor, vulnerable, and totally dependent on God. Peter now wonders what reward they will receive.

Jesus promptly responds that whoever leaves everything for love of him "and for the sake of the Gospel" will receive a hundredfold even in this life (together with persecution) and "eternal life in the age to come." Generosity opens up the heart to receive God's plentiful gifts of joy.

"Leaving everything" meant certain things for the disciples. What does "leaving everything" mean for us here and now? What will liberate our hearts to freely and unconditionally love Jesus and be a part of the kingdom of God, and to receive eternal life at the end of our journey?

Perhaps it means refusing a job that, for a Christian, would involve morally unacceptable behavior or values and accepting a job or occupation generating less pay. "Leaving everything" might invite a married couple to be open to more children, and consequently to having a less expensive car or home, or scaling back on vacations. Other ways of choosing Jesus Christ and his values could be to stand up to injustice in society; to reconcile relationships; or to tithe and perform deeds of charity for the poor, the homeless, the sick, and the imprisoned. This "leaving everything" can be the choice to set aside quality time in each day or each week to pray and worship God in the community assembly or family. Every effort we make, no matter how small, to wisely choose God's plan for us in our life will reap a hundredfold of peace and joy now, and unending joy in eternal life.

Oratio

Jesus, Lord of all and the fullness of my desiring, help me to see what you are calling me to leave for your sake and the sake of your kingdom. Help me not to focus on what I must forgo or give up, but to consider the possession of your all-surpassing love. Give me the strength to leave everything behind for your sake and the sake of the Gospel, eternal glory, and joy. Amen.

Contemplatio

"My God and my all!"

Wednesday of the Eighth Week
of Ordinary Time

⁘. . . . .⁘

Lectio

Mark 10:32–45

Meditatio

> *"Grant that in your glory we may sit
> one at your right and the other at your left."*

Bravo! What a request! Probably most people respond to James and John's petition to be at the right and left hand of Jesus in his kingdom just as the other apostles did: "How dare they? Who do they think they are? How selfish of them to try to wiggle their way into the good graces of Jesus and get to the top before *me!*" Have you ever entertained such thoughts?

It's interesting, however, that Jesus doesn't respond with a reprimand to James and John. At the end of the Gospel he addresses the reaction of the other apostles. I wonder why?

First, Jesus plays along with the two apostles' game. "Promise us you'll do whatever we ask you to do." "Okay," he responds, "what do you want?" Jesus was certainly not as serious about himself as the men who followed him were serious about themselves. He could play and write outside the lines.

I can imagine the fondness with which he receives James and John's loyal promise to drink of his chalice. How much it must warm his heart to receive this token of their love. Yes, perhaps it is a bit mixed in with ambition, but, honestly, isn't all love mixed with a bit of immaturity and dross? And, frankly, they offer Jesus their promise of loyalty to *death* (no small promise), while the other ten simply become indignant that if they hadn't been watching closely to protect their rights, the offending duo would have jockeyed into higher positions than they.

Homilies and spiritual books concentrate on Jesus' final words, "whoever wishes to be great among you will be your servant." But perhaps if the other ten hadn't started an argument, Jesus wouldn't have needed to say that. Perhaps Jesus would have just given the two ambitious apostles a brotherly pat on the back, grateful that, at least in some budding way, they had higher aspirations to live and even to *die* with him.

Oratio

Jesus, they say we receive from you as much as we believe we shall. So I'm going to the top with this request. I want to be with you forever. I ask you yourself to accomplish in me all that you desire me to be. I know you will do this for me because you love me. Amen.

Contemplatio

Accomplish in me all that you desire of me.

Thursday of the Eighth Week of Ordinary Time

:⋯⋯⋯⋯:

Lectio

Mark 10:46–52

Meditatio

"Master, I want to see."

Did you ever play childhood games in which you were blindfolded and therefore dependent on sounds and touch to know where you were? Imagine a lifetime of blindness: depending on the help of others, not seeing where you are and the beauty that surrounds you or the nonverbal communication of body language or a glance!

Bartimaeus is blind. He longs to be able to see. When he learns that Jesus is passing by, he repeatedly cries out, "Jesus, Son of David, have pity on me." His perseverance and faith are rewarded, for Jesus hears him and tells the bystanders to call Bartimaeus. When Jesus asks what he wants, the blind man replies, "Master, I want to see." And Jesus heals him.

Can we imagine what he first saw? Perhaps he first looked upon the face of Jesus. What was communicated in that gaze? Whatever Bartimaeus learned caused him to follow Jesus on the way.

We too might suffer from poor vision and wish to be able to see. Even more than physical blindness, however, we might suffer from spiritual blindness. Then our vision of success or happiness may be limited to having a good-looking body, a house filled with the latest gadgets, or a prestigious job. This blindness inhibits our ability to see God's presence in our day, or to recognize God's love and care. Our life could be so different if we had the vision of faith.

What can we do? Let us imitate Bartimaeus, recognize our blindness, and strongly desire to see. Let us turn to Jesus and cry out longingly, "Jesus, Master, I want to see!" Jesus never refuses this prayer. Bartimaeus immediately received his sight, but the spiritual vision that we seek grows gradually. As we continue to ask for this gift, we will begin to notice God's presence and action. We will come to understand life with its circumstances differently. This is the type of vision that we long for. Therefore let us repeatedly cry out, "Jesus, I want to see!"

Oratio

Jesus, when I stop to consider how I look at life, at its circumstances, and even at things, I realize that my vision is so superficial. I truly suffer from spiritual blindness. Sometimes I forget that there is more to reality. Sometimes I don't even remember you and how essential you are to me. Lord, heal my blindness, as you healed Bartimaeus. I want to see with new eyes, with faith. Grant me this vision. Reveal your presence to me today. Help me to see as you see so that I, too, can more closely follow you on the way.

Contemplatio

Lord, grant that I may truly see.

Friday of the Eighth Week
of Ordinary Time

⋮·············⋮

Lectio

Mark 11:11–26

Meditatio

> *". . . the whole crowd was astonished at his teaching."*

I am in that crowd of people who find themselves astonished as they watch and listen to Jesus in this Gospel passage.
Between yesterday and today the lectionary skipped over the
first ten verses of chapter 11, Mark's account of the trium-
phal entry into Jerusalem. Though unspoken in this liturgy
during ordinary time, the electricity of that Palm Sunday
weekend still crackles in the background. It flashes out in
Jesus' words and actions that catch me off guard.

His behavior challenges me to reevaluate some of my
kindergarten lessons: that being *good* equals being *nice*, and
nice people never get upset. Here is Jesus—goodness incarnate—beyond the stage of merely being upset. He is angry.
What provoked this? The heart of this Gospel concerns an
issue of prayer. Worship is meant to bear fruit. Those whom
God calls are to make time and space for others to join in
worship—not to place obstacles or, worse yet, to clutter that
space with business affairs. Jesus quotes a phrase from Isaiah
56:7: "My house shall be called a house of prayer for all

peoples," and he adds, quoting Jeremiah 7:11, "but you have made it a den of thieves." The temple, the church, is not a private club or a place of business; it is God's sacrament for the healing, comfort, guidance, and salvation of all people.

Jesus' anger in this Gospel challenges me to reevaluate my attitude toward prayer and worship. Allowing space for prayer, opening up to those "outside" the chosen few, letting prayer bear fruit, are all nonnegotiable for Jesus. He isn't simply making a suggestion to be considered and followed at my convenience. Jesus takes this quite personally.

Oratio

Lord, I am amazed at how quickly I become complacent in my understanding of Christianity. I become lulled by the aesthetics and the comfort of familiarity—not that there's anything wrong with those things in and of themselves—but my tendency is to close in on myself or my own little circle. When I truly allow you to be who you are, Lord, you break through the patina of "niceness" that I throw over your teaching and example. Open my eyes and my heart to see what your passionately held priorities mean for my life today. Push me out of my comfort zone into your pattern of self-giving love.

Contemplatio

Do I let Jesus' words and actions astonish me?

Saturday of the Eighth Week
of Ordinary Time

∵∴

Lectio

Mark 11:27–33

Meditatio

"If we say, 'Of heavenly origin,' he will say, 'Then why did you not believe him?' But shall we say, 'Of human origin'?"

If we are honest with ourselves, we must admit that sometimes we don't want to know the truth. We might feel angry with someone and want to stay that way. We realize that if we knew the whole story, we might have to admit that our anger is not justified, so we willfully remain in ignorance. Perhaps serious moral issues are being debated in our nation, but we don't want to read about them because then we would feel obliged to *do* something about them. So we deliberately avoid educating ourselves on certain issues.

The people who approach Jesus in this Gospel story are not being honest. At heart they don't want to know the truth, and Jesus knows their hearts. They ask him a question not to sincerely seek knowledge, but to challenge Jesus in their disbelief. In turn, he asks them a question that exposes their dishonesty, hoping to help them face it. He asks them their opinion about John the Baptist. They discuss among themselves how to respond. But they're not searching their hearts to decide what they truly think about the situation; they're searching for the most expedient response. They don't want to open themselves to criticism from Jesus (by answering that John's baptism was of God), nor to criticism from the crowd (by saying John had no higher authority).

So they come up with that most unoriginal of answers to hard questions: We don't know. It's not that they don't know; it's that they don't want to deal with the consequences of their conviction, whatever it is. It's even hard to tell what their impression of John is, since they don't even try to answer the question.

Since they show themselves to be closed to the truth about John, Jesus knows they will not be open to the truth about him. So he refuses to answer their question.

Are our hearts open to the truth about Jesus?

Oratio

Jesus, sometimes I am not completely open to the truth, either out of laziness or out of attachment to my point of view. You are the Truth, Jesus. I want to be a lover and seeker of truth, not one who seeks the easy way out. Open my eyes and my heart; help me become more and more transparent, so that my words reflect the truth about myself and I reflect the truth about you.

Contemplatio

Your face, O Lord, I seek.

Ninth Sunday of Ordinary Time — Year A

∴ · · · · · · · · · · · · ∴

Lectio

Matthew 7:21–27

Meditatio

". . . the one who does the will of my Father . . ."

With these words Jesus gave us the key to discerning which path to follow in life. But it is not so easy to apply these criteria. Sometimes others may try to entice us into following a path of evil. But usually our options are confusing because they all appear to be good to a greater or lesser extent. Becoming a nurse or a teacher are both good options. Some people do extraordinary things in the parish or school and want others to join them. Groups of friends can welcome others into their midst for social, religious, or productive reasons, all of which have good purposes. So how can we discern the will of the Father in heaven?

Here are three clues. First, the Father's will is not about outward show or splendid accomplishments. "Did we not do mighty deeds in your name?" No, we have a quiet assurance that no matter what, this is what I am meant to do, what I was born to be. I know this in the deepest core of my being where my desires meet God's desires.

Second, we find the will of God when we listen intently. Whatever we do is done because God has sent us to do it. In today's world of instant everything, many do not have the patience needed to bring to maturity their capacity to know, love, and follow God's will. We run to do, to fix, to preach out of our own nervousness, insecurity, and hubris. "Did we not prophesy in your name?" We can only securely preach to others if we have ourselves been sent by God.

Third, the will of God bathes our relationships in love. Jesus came to exorcise evil and sin from the world, but he did it by showing us the face of a loving Father and offering his life for ours. "Did we not drive out demons in your name?" Alas, we can act out of a thirst for power and with cruelty and callousness. If we are truly accomplishing the will of God our love will amaze and humble others.

Oratio

My dearest Father, I want to know your plan for me. I know it isn't a blueprint in the sky that I have to figure out. Sometimes I have to take a step into the unknown and test the waters. I believe that you will show me my place in the history of the world's salvation because I long to accomplish all you have created me to do and be for others.

Contemplatio

Show me your will, O God, and I will follow you unreservedly.

Ninth Sunday of Ordinary Time — Year B

⁘ · · · · · · · · · · · · ⁘

Lectio

Mark 2:23–3:6

Meditatio

> *"The Sabbath was made for man, not man for the Sabbath."*

Every week has its Sabbath—a day set aside, the special day among the seven. For the Jews, it is Saturday; for Christians, it is Sunday, because that is the day of Christ's resurrection. In today's society, Sunday has become simply part of the weekend, a catch-up day for shopping, cleaning, and repairing. Then there are sports, cinema, and social events. Any reminder that Sunday is the Lord's Day may be met with resistance. Jesus said, "The Sabbath was made for man, not man for the Sabbath." "We're supposed to enjoy ourselves on Sunday," we might respond.

Jesus does want us to enjoy ourselves. After all, earth's joy is a prelude to the eternal joys of heaven. However, the biggest of these joys to come will be an understanding of worship. What does it mean to worship? Will we really enjoy an eternity of adoration and praise of God? Shouldn't we start this grand eternal occupation now, during our Sunday worship? We could look at our eternal occupation as similar to the sports we play. We practice and participate in various sports in order to eventually win. We go to the field or court or links a couple of times a week in order to achieve a level of proficiency. How much time and effort do we put into praying better? In a similar fashion we could also view the question of heavenly worship by thinking of our favorite television shows. We anticipate viewing them. We give them our full attention and resent anything that might replace them. We remember the storylines and gladly discuss them with friends during the week. Shouldn't our Sunday worship also take a favored spot on the schedule of the week? The Sabbath is made for man. It is a gift from God so that we will have the opportunity to practice for and participate in the greatest event in our life: the joys of heaven.

Oratio

Lord, you accompany us through our weekly wheat fields. You defend us in our many needs, but you also remind us of our greatest need—the need to praise our God—to practice and participate in adoration as your people. Heaven awaits us with all its joy. Help us to stay focused on the final goal of this life, that we may enjoy its every moment and be prepared for eternity with you.

Contemplatio

The Sabbath was made for our joy.

Ninth Sunday of Ordinary Time—
Year C

❖· · · · · · · · · · · ·❖

Lectio

Luke 7:1–10

Meditatio

"When Jesus heard this he was amazed at him. . . ."

I once heard from a boy who was twelve or thirteen years old. He said he "came from a long line of Catholics" but his mother had abandoned the practice of the faith. In fact, he was not even baptized. He not only wanted Baptism, but he also wanted to fully participate in the life of the Church. He asked, "How can I do this?" I was amazed. How many pre-teens would have such an avid interest in their faith that they would go out of their way to receive the sacraments? It gave me hope that despite the falling away from faith on the part of many Catholics, the Church will go on because of such amazing faith that seems to spring out of nowhere.

In today's Gospel, the centurion's faith amazes Jesus. Only rarely do the Gospels say that Jesus was amazed. He marvels at this centurion, whose faith also seemed to come out of nowhere. This Gospel story shows us two sides of the centurion. The Jewish elders who approach Jesus say that the centurion is worthy to have Jesus help the ill servant. But the centurion says of himself that he is not worthy to have Jesus even visit his house. The contrast shows two different perceptions of the same man. The centurion has the virtue of humility, a virtue worth pursuing.

Humility is honesty. It is telling the truth about ourselves. Humility avoids conceit and any form of being puffed up about oneself. On the other hand, humility acknowledges the gifts that we have received from God. This virtue does not mean putting ourselves down. To refuse to recognize the gifts God has given us would not be humility but ingratitude.

Jesus is amazed at the centurion because of his humility and faith. At every Mass, we repeat the words of the centurion, "Lord, I am not worthy" to receive you. . . . We do this to admit our neediness before God, and to ask for the graces we know he will generously give us through the Holy Eucharist.

Oratio

Lord Jesus, like the centurion, I too am not worthy to approach you. But I do so full of confidence and trust in your goodness. Say but the word and I shall be healed. Jesus, you were amazed at the centurion's faith. I am amazed at your love for me. I trust in your love. Help me to grow in humility before you, acknowledging that all I have is a gift from your love.

Contemplatio

Say but the word and I will be healed.

Monday of the Ninth Week
of Ordinary Time

⁝ · · · · · · · · · · · ⁝

Lectio

Mark 12:1–12

Meditatio

"The stone that the builders rejected has become the cornerstone. . . ."

In today's Gospel, Jesus is using parables to address the chief priests, the scribes, and the elders. In my imagination, I want to see what is going on, so I walk over to where they are standing around the Master. I push my way to the center of the group so as to hear Jesus better and also to better experience the reactions of those around me.

This story of the vineyard owner is amazing. The tenants beat up his servants and yet the owner continues to trust and send other servants, finally sending his own son. Jesus tells us that the owner reasons, "They will respect my son." But the worst happens: the beloved son is shamelessly killed because of the tenants' greed and jealousy.

As Jesus finishes this parable, I hear a lot of grumbling as I stand in the midst of the leaders of the people. They have surmised that this story was aimed at them. They are incensed, turning to quickly walk away, and I am left standing, looking at Jesus. It looks as if the builders have rejected the cornerstone. Now I look at myself and ask, how many times have I walked away from the Gospel, from Christ, and from all that I desire most to be the foundation of my life?

I thank the Lord who looks at me, seeing all the possibilities for good. I wonder at the generosity of God, who ceaselessly looks for fruit in my life, in my Church, in my society. Always trusting and hoping, God loves us past the waywardness. I'd like to make God's way my way. I need to place Jesus as the cornerstone, and to be aware of all the ways he would like to gather fruit from my life today. To whom is he sending me today that I may welcome them? What fruit does God desire to gather from my life today?

Oratio

Divine Teacher, I can be rather picky at times, setting up the circumstances and parameters within which I think you must work. I can be so self-obsessed, seeing myself as central to all, ignoring what you are doing, slowly and patiently, in this world of human hearts and lives. The fruits of your Holy Spirit are "love, joy, peace, patience, kindness, generosity, faithfulness, gentleness, self-control" (Gal 5:22). Today I will live one of these in gratitude. Help me to be patient with myself and with others when we seem to bear no fruit. I trust that you are with us and know how to bring about growth in each one.

Contemplatio

You have graciously freed us from our sins by the blood of your Son.

Tuesday of the Ninth Week
of Ordinary Time

⁝ · · · · · · · · · · · ⁝

Lectio

Mark 12:13–17

Meditatio

"You do not regard a person's status. . . ."

The Pharisees and Herodians had sized up Jesus accurately—at least in this regard. Cultural anthropologists tell us that in the cosmopolitan Mediterranean world of Jesus' day, status and honor were extremely important. Yet Jesus showed no interest in them at all. This was one of the aspects of the so-called "divine reversal" that Jesus brought into the world.

Disregard for status, however, didn't catch on quickly in the Christian community. For we find both James and Paul having to admonish their flocks for choosing the first places and failing to share their sumptuous meals (see Jas 2:1–9; I Cor 11:17–22). Competition for status seems ingrained in the human psyche. Even centuries after Christ—and in a democratic society—the problem still remains.

We followers of Jesus need to be alert to the danger of striving to be successful in the eyes of others. For example, if we are doing well financially and use our money responsibly—perhaps providing for aging parents, giving our children a good education and contributing to Church and civic causes—we may believe we're doing everything we should. But what will Jesus say when we appear before him? He might ask: "How much love did you put into all that?" Someone with almost no means but more loving concern may be doing much more for his or her dependents than a person of "status" with his or her large gifts of money.

Sunday Mass can be a great leveler, especially in city parishes. *Everybody* is there. (Remember that description of the Church: "Here comes everybody!") Packed into those pews are the rich and the poor, the famous and the unknown, the educated and the simple, the descendant of the Pilgrims and the newest immigrant. Among them are many holy souls, but we don't know which ones they are.

It's food for thought.

Oratio

Jesus, it seems that status is a necessary evil in our world (perhaps an aspect of rendering to Caesar). Please help me to remember, however, that your standards are far different from those of our culture. In reality, your standards are the only ones that matter. Help me, insofar as I can, to treat each person with respect, recalling that everyone has been created in your image. Each person reflects different aspects of you. Each is like a musical note or chord, and together all of us can make a symphony.

Contemplatio

Lord, I want to shine in *your* eyes.

Wednesday of the Ninth Week
of Ordinary Time

❧ ‧‧‧‧‧‧‧‧‧‧‧‧ ❧

Lectio

Mark 12:18–27

Meditatio

> *". . . you do not know the Scriptures or the power of God."*

Jesus must have a twinkle in his eye as he patiently listens to the Sadducees and their contorted example. Marriage is a point of interest in any discussion, especially a religious one. Jesus puts all seven husbands and the poor widow to one side and tells the Sadducees exactly what they do not want to hear: "You do not know the Scriptures or the power of God." In a gentle but pointed answer, Jesus reminds them that he knows what is important in the Book of Moses—who God is for the people of Israel, a God of the living, not of the dead.

I notice that Jesus uses the present tense when he speaks of the life of those who have risen from the dead. ("When they rise . . . they neither marry nor are given in marriage . . .") The Sadducees used the future tense (". . . when they arise whose wife will she be?"). With the crowd gathered around, I feel the hint of a deep mystery in Jesus, and become aware that he is more than an itinerant preacher. His awareness is more than that of our mortal life. His thoughts move from earth to heaven with incredible ease and clarity. I wonder if his disciples and the Sadducees notice this, too.

In our day, controversies like this are not unusual; they occur whenever people mix and live together. Jesus had his share to deal with, too. Jesus answered the Sadducees with eternal truth, not with sophistry or hairsplitting. He is truly the greatest Teacher who ever set foot on this earth. We are so blessed to have his words to meditate on and make a part of ourselves.

Oratio

Lord, help me to treasure your holy word as it deserves, and to nourish my heart and soul with the wondrous message of your Gospel. I am confident and comforted in the presence of your Good News, because I know that you alone have the words of everlasting life. Teach me to remain quiet and calm in the presence of the Gospel, so that I can hear with the ears of my heart and grow.

Contemplatio

I am so blessed to have your word, Lord.

Thursday of the Ninth Week
of Ordinary Time

⁘· · · · · · · · · · · ·⁙

Lectio

Mark 12:28–34

Meditatio

"You shall love . . ."

In speaking English, we commonly use the one word "love" to express many different types of feelings and relationships: I love God, my family, the sisters in my religious community, my friends, and the people I serve through our mission. But I also love vanilla ice cream, walking in the park on a spring day, and watching a sunrise. Clearly, I have different levels of relationship with each of my "loves," and they differ greatly in their importance to me. In today's Gospel, Jesus goes to the heart of two of the most significant loves we can experience: love for God and for the people with whom we live.

Jesus presents us with a strong command to love God and our neighbor. He is not just suggesting or recommending this. Instead, Jesus requires his followers to live in love of God and neighbor. Jesus' command to love and the witness of his own life show us that love is much deeper than warm, fuzzy feelings. Love for God and neighbor means freely choosing to make a gift of ourselves even when it is difficult and calls us to make sacrifices. Jesus himself tells us, "No one has greater love than this, to lay down one's life for one's friends" (Jn 15:13).

Jesus inseparably unites the two commandments of love for God and neighbor, showing us that our love for God can never be separated from our love of neighbor. As a disciple of Jesus, each of us is called to communicate God's love to our families, our communities, and our world.

Sometimes it can feel easier for me to love God in the quiet moments of prayer, and more difficult to love my neighbor in the midst of the daily struggles of life. This Gospel is a powerful reminder to me that true love of God requires and flows into love of my neighbor.

Oratio

Jesus Master, your example and words show me how to grow in authentic love of both God and my neighbor. You show me that real love involves sacrifice and deep faith in your love for me. Help me, in my daily life, to be open to the experiences of love that you give me. May I learn from you how to love without limits or conditions, as you have loved me.

Contemplatio

"God is love, and whoever remains in love remains in God . . ." (I Jn 4:16).

Friday of the Ninth Week of Ordinary Time

∵ · · · · · · · · · · · · ∴

Lectio

Mark 12:35–37

Meditatio

"The great crowd heard this with delight."

When we hear today that the people were delighted, we think, "Oh, good, this will be a pleasant reading." But is that what happened? Jesus seems instead to be looking for some controversy. The scribes have claimed that the Messiah is David's son. Of course, we know that this is true because Jesus was born in the family of David. However, Jesus asks how the scribes can propose this since David himself, under the inspiration of the Holy Spirit, calls the Messiah his Lord. How could a great king such as David bow to a descendant yet to come? Jesus has quoted to the people from Psalm 110, one of their favorites, attributed to King David. They hear a praise of their greatest king and the promise of their coming liberation through a future leader. Their joy rises at the thought that this mysterious teacher before them might himself be the Messiah-king. Maybe he is announcing himself through images known to the people, but obscure to the occupying enemy. That is clever, they may be thinking. It will be a surprise for the hated Roman invaders.

Rather than a controversy with the scribes, Jesus is actually revealing a prophecy within a prophetic psalm. He wants his hearers, and perhaps especially the well-educated scribes, to reflect on what David had foretold about the promised Messiah. He will not just be a great conqueror who will free the oppressed people from their enemies, but he will also free them from their worst enemy: sin. He will be not only an ideal king, but also the giver of the law of love. He will also be a priest, but not, as their priests do, offering grains and the blood of animals. The Messiah-priest will offer a sacrifice of his own body and blood not just for reparation, but also as mystic food sustaining his kingdom forever. Jesus is planting inspiration for them to reflect on as God's plan unfolds in their midst. The hope is that they, too, will declare him Lord.

Oratio

Dear Lord, with my whole heart and soul I proclaim you my Messiah, King, Prophet, and Priest. Keep me open to your law, which teaches sincere love of you and my neighbor; lead me by your power to serve in humility; incorporate me into your sacrifice so that I may join you in your selfless gift to the heavenly Father. Let my whole life be a prophecy of the kingdom present among us in the Church and coming in the future glory. Amen.

Contemplatio

May I always proclaim you Lord.

Saturday of the Ninth Week
of Ordinary Time

⁘ · · · · · · · · · · · ⁘

Lectio

> Mark 12:38–44

Meditatio

> "... *this poor widow put in more*
> *than all the other contributors to the treasury* ..."

How can two small coins worth a few cents be more than the "large sum" the rich put in? This gives us a marvelous glimpse into God's heart. For God looks at the giver's love and trust rather than the gift's monetary value. He sees our motivation. Jesus criticizes those scribes who perform their religious duties to receive human praise. This poor widow, instead, in her humble, hidden way, is giving from her heart all she has, only to please God. She receives no human benefit from her giving.

But God, who sees all, regards her faith. She has given everything she has to live on, believing that God will take care of her. Or perhaps she isn't even thinking of the future. God is everything to her. She has received all from him and gives all back to him in an exchange of pure love. She lives these words of Scripture: "My portion is the Lord, says my soul; therefore will I hope in him" (Lam 3:24). She is among those blessed souls who have discovered in their poverty that when they have nothing but God, God is enough.

This is also an occasion to praise not only the mercy but the justice of God. He never asks more of us than what he has given. He is well aware of our weakness and poverty—not only material, but also spiritual. Everything we have is on loan from God. If we use it for his glory we will find joy and fulfillment. If, on the other hand, we seek our happiness in material goods we will find neither happiness nor fulfillment.

By calling the disciples to observe the widow, Jesus is inviting them and us to see things in a new way: to see things the way God sees them, to take on a new set of values, to live in the kingdom where spiritual goods outrank material goods, where the love with which we do something raises it to an infinite value.

Oratio

Dear Lord, help me to keep my eyes fixed on you. Help me to see things the way you see them. Give me a generous heart, so that I may be able to give myself to others, to share my time and my talents, trusting that you will multiply the good done and you will take care of me and my family. Give me a pure heart that seeks to give only for love of you, not for the sake of human praise or gratitude. Live and act in me so that the good I do may bear fruit for eternal life.

Contemplatio

"Blessed are you who are poor, for the kingdom of God is yours" (Lk 6:20).

Tenth Sunday of Ordinary Time — Year A

∴⋯⋯⋯⋯∴

Lectio

Matthew 9:9–13

Meditatio

"He said to him, 'Follow me.' And he got up and followed him."

In this Gospel passage Jesus invites another disciple to follow him. Just as he called his first disciples while they were tending to their chores as fishermen, so also he calls Matthew at his post where he made his living. He is a tax collector, an occupation well known for abuses and collaboration with the Romans. So his fellow Jews regard Matthew as a sinner. Regardless of what others think, Matthew accepts Jesus' invitation to leave his past behind and follow him.

It was well known that Jesus ate and conversed with tax collectors and sinners. When Matthew becomes a disciple, he invites all his friends to enjoy a meal with Jesus. On seeing such a group gathering around him, some Pharisees complain that by associating with them, Jesus is making himself ritually impure. They believe that in order to meet God's expectations and receive favors from him, one must follow rules and regulations of the Mosaic Law to the letter. Motivations do not seem to matter as long as one is self-sufficiently just. These Pharisees see themselves in this category. They consider anyone not meeting these criteria to be a sinner and hopelessly lost.

They do not know who Jesus is, nor do they understand that he is taking the opportunity to draw sinners to repentance and offer them spiritual healing. In explaining his association with sinners, Jesus quotes from the prophet Hosea, through whom God said to unfaithful Israel: "For it is love that I desire, not sacrifice, and knowledge of God rather than holocausts" (Hos 6:6). Jesus knows that human beings are weak, fragile, and fallen. What matters most to him is where one's heart is. Knowledge of and love for him, as well as one's neighbor, are more important than rigid observation of human rules and self-imposed sacrifices.

Oratio

Every day you call me, Jesus, to follow you in faith. In whatever daily duty or task at hand, you invite me to keep my focus on you. I thank you for accepting me as I am; weak, fragile, and fallen. You are my hope, and I look to you for healing. I need your merciful love; draw me to yourself so that I may repent of my sins and follow you, wherever you lead me. Help me to be compassionate toward my neighbors, my companions on my earthly journey, so they too may know of your merciful love.

Contemplatio

"I desire mercy, not sacrifice."

Tenth Sunday of Ordinary Time — Year B

:•············•:

Lectio

> Mark 3:20–35

Meditatio

> *"Here are my mother and my brothers. For whoever does
> the will of God is my brother and sister and mother."*

This passage starts out with Jesus' being at home as a large crowd gathers. His relatives hear of this and "set out to seize him." The passage ends with the arrival of the relatives and Jesus' remarks to them. In between, Mark places the account of the unbelieving scribes from Jerusalem.

As I read this entire passage, it seems to be a patchwork, but as I meditate, something that appears as a backdrop comes into focus for me. It is all about Jesus and relationships. Jesus tells us the deepest basis of all relationships: believing in one another; being ready to go the extra mile to do God's will together; sharing life and faith under the gaze of the heavenly Father, whose sons and daughters we are.

Jesus struggles to make this clear to the scribes, whose declarations he does not hesitate to call blasphemies. Jesus is unyielding, and he says blasphemy against the Holy Spirit is an unforgivable sin. To accuse Jesus of casting out Satan by the power of Satan does not make sense. Even more, it is making a sham of Jesus' mission to come and put us into right relationship with the Father in the Holy Spirit.

Mark places the people who were closest to Jesus as witnesses of this blasphemy, perhaps to make us aware of how deeply this careless and evil talk hurt our Savior. I place myself in that little knot of relatives who came to take Jesus aside to rest, and hear the sharp intake of breath as they listen to this bitter attack on Jesus' very reason for coming. I think I begin to understand better what holy hours for reparation mean, how precious they must be to the heart of the Savior.

Oratio

Lord Jesus, my heart breaks with yours to hear your loving incarnation cast into the dust by careless and callous people. I see how you turn from that tense standoff to take comfort in those who are your relatives, and those who have become your brothers and sisters and mothers through the trust they have placed in you. I want to stand with you always, and ask you to support my weak faith with the grace you came to bring us through your death and resurrection. Amen.

Contemplatio

" . . . my brother and sister and mother. . . ."

Tenth Sunday of Ordinary Time —
Year C

∴ · · · · · · · · · · · · ∴

Lectio

Luke 7:11–17

Meditatio

> *"When the Lord saw her, he was moved with pity . . ."*

In today's Gospel, two crowds converge as Jesus reaches the city gates of Nain with his disciples: a large *crowd* with him, and the *crowd* accompanying a widow burying her only son. The sheer number of people evokes an image of noise, emotion, and confusion. The stage is set and our attention is fixed on the two central figures: Jesus and the grieving widow.

The Master's sensitive heart immediately grasps the depth of the widow's pain and anguish. Looking directly at her, Jesus approaches the coffin, gently saying, "Do not weep." The crowd grows still and the bearers halt as Jesus, touching the coffin commands: "Young man, I tell you, arise!"

To the crowd's astonishment, Jesus rebukes death and restores life. The dead man gets up and Jesus gives him to his mother. She and all those with her are overwhelmed with amazement and fear even as they glorify God and exclaim: "A great prophet has arisen in our midst!"

This miracle is reminiscent of that performed by the prophet Elisha for the Shunammite woman whose young son had also mysteriously died and been raised (see 2 Kgs 4:18–37), or that of the prophet Elijah for the widow of Zarephath (see 1 Kgs 17:17–24). In each incident the prophet had ardently invoked the Lord God to restore life. Here instead, we see Jesus as conqueror of death, acting in his own name and with his own divine power. In his human heart, Jesus was moved to divine compassion, which restored wholeness and wellness to both soul and body of the young man.

What a wonderful meeting those two crowds (the one accompanying the Author of Life and the other led by death) witnessed that day! Their encounter leads them to bear witness to all they have seen and heard as they go home rejoicing, knowing that truly this day, "God has visited his people!"

Oratio

Jesus, breathe into my soul the newness of your life, that I may share always more deeply in your divine life. Let others come to know your love through every word and action of mine. Teach me, Jesus, to let my heart be deeply moved with compassion for all those who taste the bitterness of grief and pain. Help me to be a bearer of light and of faith, comfort, and hope, even when sorrow or despair threatens to prevail. Speak your words of wisdom and healing, so that with renewed hope and courage we may follow you in all things and eagerly serve the needs of one another in love.

Contemplatio

"Because I live . . . you will live" (Jn 14:19).

Monday of the Tenth Week of Ordinary Time

∵ · · · · · · · · · · · · ∴

Lectio

Matthew 5: 1–12

Meditatio

"He began to teach them."

How do you feel when you look over the edge of a cliff or the ledge of a tall building? Do you feel dizzy? Do you feel thrilled to look out over a beautiful vista or at the tiny cars and people below? Or do you feel fear at such a great height and back away to safety? Reading the Beatitudes can make us feel much the same as being on a height with an amazing view. They are a bold challenge to our instinct for self-preservation!

Living the Beatitudes means to forget myself and live for others. This is harder than it sounds, but more rewarding than I could ever imagine. When Jesus tells his disciples, "Whoever finds his life will lose it, and whoever loses his life for my sake will find it" (Mt 10:39), he is summarizing the Beatitudes.

Each Beatitude calls me to lose my life in some way. To obtain the blessedness that Jesus describes I need to let go of grudges, of desiring revenge, of setting my heart on things I don't need. I must let go of the security of being a silent bystander when others call for help or need a caring word, perhaps at the risk of being persecuted. Each one of us is called to live the Beatitudes in a unique way. I have to search my heart and find that place where I feel dizzy or faint in my spirit. That is where the Beatitudes need to take effect!

The teaching of the Beatitudes is truly Good News coming from God himself: "He began to teach them. . . ." Jesus is teaching us how to become fully human, in the image of our Divine Creator. When I falter before his teaching and want to back away from the view, I remember that Jesus is the Word of God and he has power to transform my inner being. By his word he can bring a beautiful creation out of the chaos of my life. In Christ, I can climb to the heights and live the Beatitudes.

Oratio

Jesus, you are the Divine Teacher. You spoke the Beatitudes so they would take root in my heart, not just remain on paper. With you I desire to contemplate the heights to which the Beatitudes call me, and to experience in my life today the joy of letting go of my desires so I can live for others.

Contemplatio

Jesus, teach me your way of truth and holiness.

Tuesday of the Tenth Week
of Ordinary Time

⁘ · · · · · · · · · · · · ⁘

Lectio

Matthew 5:13–16

Meditatio

"But if salt loses its taste . . ."

I have to admit that sometimes my "salt" goes flat. It loses
its taste. I'm not talking about my table salt—I'm talking about
me. Sometimes I'm tired. I'm sick. I just don't care. I wonder if
it's all worth it. If we're honest, these times come to all of us.
In fact, they are a normal part of development. If I keep a rub-
ber band stretched out, it will eventually break. If we are running at top speed all the time, we will crack. Sometimes salt
goes flat, lights are hidden under the bushel baskets of life, and
only faintly burning embers keep the fire alive.

However, that isn't what Jesus is talking about when he
preaches about the salt. It isn't feelings, energy, or health. A
Jew hearing Jesus talk about salt would know that Jesus is
talking about how the Jews were to be a living covenant. By
living that covenant with God, they would draw all peoples
and nations to worship their God and adore him. All sacrifices offered in the temple were sprinkled with salt as a
reminder that God's covenant was everlasting and could never
be revoked or reneged on.

So when Jesus tells his disciples, "*You* are the salt of the earth," he is saying that they themselves are to be the reminder of God's faithfulness. They themselves are to be the ones through whom God will draw all peoples into relationship with him.

If bringing people closer to God means all will go smoothly, all plans will succeed, and we will be perfect, then Jesus' life, Peter's life, Paul's life wouldn't make sense. They grew tired. The apostles made mistakes. Jesus wept over Jerusalem because its people hadn't accepted his message or his love. And all three died as seeming failures. But all of them lived as witnesses to the fidelity of God and his love for us. In all the twists and turns of life, salty living means the absolute certainty that God will be faithful to us. That is all. That is everything.

Oratio

Jesus, give me the courage to proclaim you with salty living, with radiant light in my family, among my friends, in my place of employment, and in my parish. When things go wrong, help me to offer a word of trust in you; when things are tough, a word of hope; when things are joyful, a word of thanksgiving.

Contemplatio

Make my life both salt and light today, my Lord.

Wednesday of the Tenth Week
of Ordinary Time

᛭ ⋯⋯⋯⋯ ᛭

Lectio

Matthew 5:17–19

Meditatio

> *"Do not think that I have come to abolish the law or the prophets.*
> *I have come not to abolish but to fulfill."*

Jesus has just begun his public life in Galilee. Now he begins the Sermon on the Mount, teaching his disciples. They have followed him up the mountain and are seated before him, eager to hear all he has to say. Unlike all the other teachers they have heard, he speaks with real authority and conviction.

Jesus speaks to them of the Law, something with which every Jew is familiar, for the Law guides and directs their lives. It is for them a summary of all wisdom, a sure way to God. Jesus tells his eager and attentive audience that he has come not to do away with this guidepost, but instead to fulfill it. "Do not think that I have come to abolish the law or the prophets. I have come not to abolish but to fulfill."

This is startling news! In what way does he fulfill the Law, the Law given through Moses on Mount Sinai, this Law that has guided their people for centuries? How can he possibly deliver on this amazing claim?

Jesus does so first by living the Law perfectly himself. He is a faithful and observant Jew. He goes to the synagogue regularly and to the Temple for all Jewish feasts. But Jesus does more—he not only lives the Law perfectly with all of its prescriptions and rituals, but he also is himself the Law. He is the Law because he is "the Way," the only way that leads to God the Father. There is no other. "I am the way and the truth and the life. No one comes to the Father except through me" (Jn 14:6). Thus Jesus is the sure guide that every Jew, and every sincere seeker with an open heart, desires to follow. Thus he is my Law, my Way, too.

Jesus is not only the Way, but he also reveals the face of the Father, who is love. And it is in allowing this God of love to live and act in us that the Law is fulfilled in our own times.

Oratio

Live in me, Jesus. Live and love in me so that your law will be fulfilled in and through my life. You who are our Way to the Father, be my Way and sure guide. Give me the grace to model my life on yours so that I might become a way for my brothers and sisters.

Contemplatio

"I am the way and the truth and the life. No one comes to the Father except through me."

Thursday of the Tenth Week
of Ordinary Time

∴ · · · · · · · · · · · · ∴

Lectio

Matthew 5:20–26

Meditatio

> ". . . *whoever says, 'You fool,' will be liable. . . .*"

When we were children, we used to respond to name-calling by chanting: "Sticks and stones may break my bones, but names can never hurt me." But of course, being called a name really did hurt. Children are probably more thoughtless than heartless. At a certain age, they seem fascinated by plays on words and they extend this wordplay to the names and traits of their peers.

As adults, hopefully, we no longer call people names. But we might *think* them. We might categorize others, labeling them mentally.

I wasn't aware that I was labeling—and that it shouldn't be done—until I heard or read something on the topic. Then I understood that, of course, it isn't good to label, because assigning labels influences our attitudes, even if we never voice our thoughts.

It would be different if we were pinning a *good* label on someone, but that's not usually the case!

Now when I find myself categorizing someone unfavorably, I try to correct myself by thinking: "That's _____," and I mentally say the person's name. He or she isn't a category but an individual, precious in God's eyes.

This passage of Matthew is dense with moral exhortation. Jesus says so much in so few words! For example, the exhortation to leave one's gift at the altar and go to become reconciled needs no comment. It's crystal clear.

Oratio

Jesus, Divine Master, your teachings on anger are clear. Please help me to remember them in times of agitation. I want to focus on the respect due to every human person. Sometimes it's hard to remember that all of us are made in your image and likeness, but I intend to keep trying.

I recall the example of Pope John Paul II, who focused on each individual as if she or he were the only person in the world. For him, there were no labels, only precious individuals, unique and unrepeatable, unconditionally loved by you, Lord.

Contemplatio

I want to appreciate the mystery of each person.

Friday of the Tenth Week of Ordinary Time

⁘ ⋯⋯⋯⋯ ⁘

Lectio

Matthew 5:27–31

Meditatio

"'You shall not commit adultery.'. . . everyone who looks at a woman with lust has already committed adultery with her in his heart . . . whoever marries a divorced woman commits adultery."

This passage begins with Jesus reiterating the known Law: "You shall not commit adultery. . . ." But to this Jesus adds that one must avoid not only adultery but also adulterous desires. In other words, not only the visible social evil is to be avoided, but also whatever might contaminate the heart or impede the beauty and truth of love. (Certainly we know that the words of Jesus, "If your right eye causes you to sin, tear it out and throw it away," are not meant to be taken literally. This hyperbole was used to emphasize how conjugal love is so precious that one is ready to give up anything to preserve it.)

The teaching of Jesus on adultery and divorce may appear to be hard, but in reality it protects and fosters true love. God inscribed in each of our hearts the capacity for love and communion, and with this gift we take on a responsibility.

The union that exists in marriage is so precious in the eyes of God that he desires to protect it, embrace it, and bless it.

This brings about a deeper harmony not only for the married couple but for all of society. The spouses have given themselves definitively and totally to each other, and God in his fidelity blesses that which has been joined together.

Human love is not to be viewed as something temporary or a passing whim. Love is not a gratifying experience or an experiment, but a serious commitment that demands the total and definitive gift of the lover. God guards and protects this kind of love with his own faithful love.

Oratio

Dear God, teach me how to love. "Love" is a worn-out word in our society. It is often portrayed as a simple need or self-centered satisfaction, yet your love is eternal, faithful, self-giving. Your love is not temporary or conditional. Teach me to love with a pure heart, and to be ready to let go of anything so as to preserve love's true meaning.

I pray also for couples who are struggling to remain faithful, especially married people who find themselves alone because of the infidelity of a spouse.

Contemplatio

Blessed are the pure of heart, for they shall see God.

Saturday of the Tenth Week
of Ordinary Time

∴ · · · · · · · · · · · · ∴

Lectio

Matthew 5:33–37

Meditatio

"Let your 'Yes' mean 'Yes,' and your 'No' mean 'No.'"

Jesus is asking his disciples, and he asks us, too, to *live* in the truth, so we will have no need for oaths. As a part of the Sermon on the Mount, this injunction of Jesus takes on added solemnity. If I were in the crowd on that day, I would probably notice the silence that seems to settle over the people as Jesus speaks these words. Who has not told a lie, little or big, seriously or jokingly?

I look at our society today and see what it means to manipulate truth to one's own advantage. Advertisements, contracts, tax laws, and even marriage oaths are sometimes written with loopholes one can use to wriggle loose from a commitment. One can slip through a loophole instead of upholding one's word when that would mean sacrifice, inconvenience, or loss of money. So often the sad injustices of our world take off from the launch pad of untruth.

Then I look within my heart to see if what I say or promise reflects what I think or intend. I have to bow my head in sorrow for the "social" lies, the little white lies, and the vague euphemisms that I, as a member of this society, may have committed, ignored, or condoned.

The most vulnerable of our society, the children and the aged, seem to be the ones who suffer the most from untruth. I try to imagine what happiness and relief they would have if they could know for certain that they will be given what they are promised, and will receive what is their due . . . .

An atmosphere of truth is the only place where real security and justice can flourish. It is important enough for Jesus to remind me with his immortal words that I must stand in the truth or not at all.

Oratio

Good Master, you teach me the way to the kingdom. I see by your clear teaching that I have to work on my own failings before I can be free enough to walk with joy and love on that way. Redeemer, help me to understand my place in the world and to walk in it with humility and trust, confident that you will guide me when I waver and help me up when I fall.

Contemplatio

Lord, may my words always ring true.

Eleventh Sunday of Ordinary Time — Year A

:·············:·

Lectio

Matthew 9:36–10:8

Meditatio

"Jesus' heart was moved with pity . . ."

This Gospel scene gives us a glimpse into the human heart of Jesus overflowing with compassion and love. "At the sight of the crowds, Jesus' heart was moved with pity for them because they were troubled and abandoned, like sheep without a shepherd." In the eyes of the people assembled before him, he recognizes their eagerness, their longing for a secure guide who can lead them to restful waters of peace.

The image of "sheep without a shepherd," takes us back to the brief but consoling Psalm 23—a psalm full of wonderful metaphors about the Lord who guides us, walks alongside us, protects us, lavishes abundant blessings on us, and fills us with all that is good. Shepherd imagery is often used in both the Old and New Testaments. In the Gospels, Jesus is the Good Shepherd who knows each person by name. He protects and searches for those who lose their way. He ultimately gives his life for us.

This succinct portrayal of Jesus' pity for the crowds is one of many occasions when the Gospel writers speak of Jesus' emotions. When he walked among us as a man, he lived a fully human life, and experienced the same sentiments as all human beings do. He felt compassion, love, agony, anger, sorrow, joy. In this sense, he is familiar with what we go through in life.

When we speak to him in prayer, expressing our thoughts and feelings with honesty and trust, Jesus is not aloof to our human experience. Even our strong emotions don't surprise him. He understands. He accepts us. He loves us.

Oratio

Lord Jesus, you are the good Master whom I wish to follow. You know my heart, my thoughts, and my emotions—the joyful, the difficult and everything in between. I want to share everything in conversation with you.

Contemplatio

Today I want to see others through the eyes of Jesus— eyes of compassion and goodness.

Eleventh Sunday of Ordinary Time — Year B

❖ · · · · · · · · · · · · ❖

Lectio

Mark 4:26–34

Meditatio

"Through it all the seed would sprout . . ."

The mustard bush is a fast-growing plant that springs up like the pesky weeds in our yards and gardens. The comparison of the kingdom to the mustard seed would be, in a sense, like comparing the kingdom to dandelions. They inevitably spring up. No matter how much you try to eliminate them, they always return, unless you make a concerted, consistent, daily effort to eradicate them.

It is a comfort to know that the kingdom is that strong.

It is invisible. Jesus didn't compare the kingdom to an olive tree, but rather to a commonplace shrub.

It is mysterious. Jesus says it comes from the smallest of seeds and somehow takes root like seeds sown by the hands of a farmer.

It springs up with little effort. We don't have to wait for it to appear, plan for it, organize it, or create strategies for its growth. It is here. The kingdom grows quickly.

It is where? Invisible, mysterious, with little effort. . . .

That sounds like the Incarnation. That sounds like the poor, the oppressed, the terminally ill, the ones taken advantage of, marginalized, unjustly treated.

"Whatever you did for one of these least brothers of mine, you did for me" (Mt 25:40). The kingdom of God is a powerless power that will overturn the world, disperse the arrogant of mind and heart, cast down the rulers from their thrones, and send the rich away empty (see Lk 1:51–53).

Are you as sure of the kingdom's growth as you are of the dandelions? If not, wake up to it all around you in hidden places. Reverence it there. Serve it there. Live it there.

Oratio

Jesus, your kingdom sometimes frightens me. In the world we learn to climb the ladder to the top. In your kingdom you teach us to descend the ladder to the bottom, just as you emptied yourself completely to become man and then to die on the cross. Help me overcome the fear of living differently, so that I can witness to the peace of inner dependence on you. Increase my faith that you will provide for me in all things, so that I will be part of the inevitable springing up of the kingdom.

Contemplatio

Thank you, Lord. Thy kingdom come.

Eleventh Sunday of Ordinary Time — Year C

⁓ · · · · · · · · · · · · ⁓

Lectio

Luke 7:36—8:3

Meditatio

> *"Simon, I have something to say to you."* . . .*"Tell me, teacher."*

If Simon is clueless, Jesus speedily enlightens him. And what a comparison he draws! No water for Jesus' feet, but those feet had now been bathed with tears. No kiss of greeting from Simon, but many kisses planted on Jesus' feet by the woman. No anointing of Jesus' head by Simon, but now an effusive anointing of his feet.

Simon is amazed to hear the teacher tell the woman, "Your sins are forgiven . . . . Your faith has saved you; go in peace." As she rises and leaves, we can imagine a stunned silence in the room, and then the buzz of incredulous conversation . . . . At this point, Simon may have been sorry. At least, he must have regretted inviting this controversial rabbi to dinner!

This incident may remind us of Jesus' parable of the prodigal son. The woman could parallel the wasteful son, and Simon the haughty brother.

Whom do I most resemble?

If I identify more with the woman/prodigal, I can rejoice. My sorrow is pleasing to the Lord. I can "go in peace."

If I identify more with Simon/elder brother, I have some serious soul-searching to do: Why am I so quick to judge my brothers and sisters? How can I question their actions and motives when I've never walked in their shoes? How can I think I'm better than they are—perhaps even believe that I'm dearer to the Lord?

It would be good to pause and reflect for a while, reviewing and revising my way of thinking about the various people in my life.

Oratio

Jesus, Lord, have mercy on me! Forgive my complacency, my easy judgments of my brothers and sisters. Help me to remember that I don't know their histories, their weaknesses, their temptations, their struggles, their victories. Help me to recognize that I'm capable of doing far worse than anything I can imagine of them. There, but for your grace, go I. Thank you for the times you have saved me from myself, perhaps when I didn't even know that I was headed for ruin. You have been so good to me! I want to become more worthy of your love.

Contemplatio

I'm sorry, Lord. Forgive me, please.

Monday of the Eleventh Week
of Ordinary Time

⁑· · · · · · · · · · ·⁑

Lectio

Matthew 5:38–42

Meditatio

> *". . . offer no resistance to one who is evil."*

This is a hard teaching, or perhaps we should say it is a difficult teaching, a challenging teaching. When we read all of chapter 5 we realize that this is part of the Sermon on the Mount. This sermon comes near the beginning of Jesus' preaching. It develops in a prepared way—rather than spontaneously—and it contains the core message of Christianity.

We should not be concerned about the origin of each of these teachings or whether they were given as one whole sermon or collected later by Matthew. Instead let us set ourselves to listen attentively. This Gospel passage is an explanation of the overall theme of love. Jesus is dismantling the common, strong inclination to seek retaliation, to exact revenge. So often we follow this lower instinct that requires nothing of our human nature—simply anger, brute force, animal cunning, "inner evil." Although we might feel strong, crafty, in control, even justified, when we retaliate we are simply acting out of animal instinct.

Jesus wants us to stand before him, to stand also in our own presence, to reflect on what has angered us—usually it is something small: an insult, a slap, a demand. Why lower ourselves to a reaction similar to the insult? If we are the better person, shouldn't our reaction be nobler? If someone wants something that is yours, give it rather than fall into a battle over it. If someone demands a service, give it willingly and even exceed the demand; give more. At the end Jesus suggests a way to ready ourselves for these difficult, demanding moments. He says, give to one who asks, do not deny one who wants to borrow. If we follow his advice our hearts will be big enough and our spirits strong enough to meet insult, injustice, and injury more gently, with nobility, with love as Jesus himself, the Son of God, met the great personal offense of his passion.

Oratio

Jesus, my God and my example, you constantly met with insult, antagonism, and pressure as you went about preaching divine love and forgiveness. Your whole mission was centered on us—on our salvation. Make my heart similar to yours, meek and humble, that what I desire for every other person will be similar to what you desire—peace in this life and eternal happiness in the next. Amen.

Contemplatio

Do not say no to kindness.

Tuesday of the Eleventh Week of Ordinary Time

❖ · · · · · · · · · · · · ❖

Lectio

Matthew 5:43–48

Meditatio

". . . love your enemies . . ."

If we could vote Gospel passages "off the island," like so many contestants in a reality show, this one would probably rank right next to Jesus' teachings about divorce. It's something we might just wish away. Experiences of enormous evil, of real, sworn enemies, can make us dismiss the whole teaching as impossible, even on a small, personal level. Adding in "be perfect, just as your Heavenly Father is perfect" magnifies the impossibility. Jesus can't really mean that, can he? Or is Jesus saying precisely what he means?

What if Jesus is telling us to be *magnanimous*, to show our family resemblance as children of the Heavenly Father? Far from measuring out every favor, God lets his rain fall on the just and the unjust. Rather than dole out our mercies, we ought to be prodigal with them. Saint Paul even spelled it out for the early Christians: "Be kind to one another, compassionate, forgiving one another as God has forgiven you in Christ" (Eph 4:32). Later in that same letter to the Ephesians, he calls us to be *"imitators of God, as beloved children"* (5:1).

Maybe it is easier to interpret that "be perfect" in terms of flawlessness, a goal we can dismiss out of hand. Instead, Jesus tells us *to be like God* in open-heartedness, and to let that goodness spread far and wide.

Oratio

Lord, inspire me to face the difficult characters at work, the aggressive drivers on the commute, and other daily "enemies" with the kindness, compassion, and spirit of forgiveness that Saint Paul described (and surely had to practice himself). Here and now I lift them up to you, whoever they are, whatever the source of their unwelcome behavior. By your grace, I want to forgive them in advance for whatever inconvenience, fright, or harm they cause me. Live in me, Jesus our Redeemer, to the glory of God the Father.

Contemplatio

"So be imitators of God, as beloved children, and live in love" (Eph 5:1–2).

Wednesday of the Eleventh Week of Ordinary Time

∵∴ · · · · · · · · · · · ·∴∵

Lectio

Matthew 6:1–6, 16–18

Meditatio

> *"Take care not to perform righteous deeds*
> *in order for people to see them . . ."*

This is the same Gospel reading that we hear every year on Ash Wednesday. But the Church wants us to reflect on our fasting, prayer, and almsgiving all year long, not just in Lent.

Matthew gives examples of people doing good things, but for the wrong reason. The motivation behind the deed is as important as the deed itself, an important point we need to reflect on. Today, we don't often blow a trumpet or pray out loud on the street corner, but we have plenty of other ways to show off.

When examining ourselves in this area, however, we need to consider something important. In our secular North American society, public displays of faith and religious expression are often frowned upon. We are free to practice religion, but are expected to keep it to ourselves and not "impose" it on other people. This isolation of religion as one piece of our private lives gradually gives God less of an influence in the public sphere.

We should never give to charity or pray or sacrifice *in order for* people to see, hoping that others will notice and admire us. But public expressions of faith can give witness to Christ in a secular world. So it might be good to pray grace before meals in a restaurant, or wear a crucifix or medal of Mary, or make the sign of the cross while passing a church where Jesus is present in the Blessed Sacrament. We don't practice our faith to make a good impression, but neither should we hide it to make a good impression.

Oratio

Jesus, sometimes I might act as if you are just one part of my life—an important one, but only one of many. In fact, you *are* my life. Without you, I would not only lose all meaning and happiness, I would also lose my life itself. I would no longer exist. Help me search my heart to see my motivations, especially in the things I consider "good deeds." Why do I do these things? Am I trying to make myself look good? Or am I trying to make you known? May my witness and example invite others to a closer relationship with you.

Contemplatio

Let them think of you, Jesus.

Thursday of the Eleventh Week of Ordinary Time

❖ · · · · · · · · · · · · ❖

Lectio

Matthew 6:7–15

Meditatio

"Our Father . . ."

In today's Gospel, Jesus, the master pray-er, teaches us how to pray. In this lesson, he shows us the connection between prayer and our relationships. He assures us that we do not need to multiply words in order to be heard, for the simple yet profound reason that God is "your Father [who] knows what you need before you ask him." Yes! God is our Father! As our Parent, God loves us and takes care of us. Would our relationship with God be different if we believed more deeply that he is our loving and caring Father?

Jesus then teaches us to pray, "Our Father . . ." With this single word, "our," Jesus reveals our relationship with one another. God is *our* Father; we are all sisters and brothers. What a vast family we have—siblings everywhere! Everyone we read about in the newspaper or pass on the street is our sister or brother. Everyone with whom we live or work is our sister or brother.

This truth can change the way we regard and treat one another. With this faith vision, we recognize others as our brothers and sisters, worthy of love and respect. Then, peace and harmony can flourish among us. It is not surprising, however, that our human weaknesses get in the way and damage or break our relationships. Thankfully, Jesus gives us the key to healing these relationships: forgiveness. He also stresses how important forgiveness is when he teaches us that our heavenly Father will forgive us only if we forgive one another.

Sometimes it can seem impossible to forgive or to ask for forgiveness. Our only recourse is prayer: asking God for the grace. We might even need to ask for the grace to want to forgive. We can trust that God will hear our prayer. Gradually we will begin to be able to forgive others or to ask for forgiveness. Our relationships with God and with others will deepen and flourish.

Oratio

Jesus, when you taught us how to pray you also revealed how connected we are to our heavenly Father and to one another. Thank you! What a gift to be a child of the Father and a brother or sister to everyone. I do not always remember that we are related, and I need your help to acquire this wonderful faith vision. At times I do not treat others with love and respect. Please give me the grace to ask forgiveness and to forgive others when they hurt me. May our unity and love flourish so that we may experience a foretaste of heavenly love.

Contemplatio

Our Father, fill my heart with love and forgiveness.

Friday of the Eleventh Week
of Ordinary Time

∴∴∴∴∴∴∴∴∴∴∴

Lectio

Matthew 6:19–23

Meditatio

"The lamp of the body is the eye."

Today's Gospel presents the image of an eye that "glows" and sheds light outwardly and inwardly. Commentaries describe the luminous eye as healthy and clear. They also identify it with a sincere and generous person. The opposite is true of the "darkened" eye. The person in whom darkness prevails is devious and stingy.

The passage begins with Jesus' exhortation to store up treasures for ourselves in heaven. Because the image of the luminous eye follows immediately, there seems to be an intimate connection: we store up heavenly wealth by being what the glowing eye implies: sound, sincere, and generous.

In our time and culture we don't use categories of light and darkness or white and black as much as intermediate shades. So, how "bright" is my eye? How "radiant" am I?

Psalm 112 has a related image that helps me to understand the ideal more completely and make an application to my life. This psalm praises the upright, generous person or persons:

"They shine through the darkness, a light for the upright; they are gracious, merciful, and just. All goes well for those gracious in lending, who conduct their affairs with justice. . . . Their hearts are tranquil, without fear, till at last they look down on their foes. Lavishly they give to the poor; their prosperity shall endure forever" (Ps 112:4–5, 8–9).

The psalm focuses on the persons described in the Beatitudes—those who strive to be all of God and suitably detached from "things." They resemble Jesus himself, for the Beatitudes have been described as a portrait of the Master.

May I learn to live always more according to the spirit of the Beatitudes!

Oratio

Holy Spirit, help me to be a true person of the Beatitudes, poor in spirit, with my life centered on the kingdom. Increase in me the gifts you gave me at Baptism and Confirmation. These gifts will make me more attuned to your inspirations, like the strings of an instrument ready to respond to the touch of a master musician. Play a beautiful melody on these strings. May my whole being resonate with the song in the heart of Jesus—the One who lived the Beatitudes perfectly.

I want to bring Jesus to others through the witness of my life, but I would never be able to do it without you. Be my inspirer, guide, and strength. Amen.

Contemplatio

I want to shine.

Saturday of the Eleventh Week of Ordinary Time

⁘ ⋯⋯⋯⋯ ⁘

Lectio

Matthew 6:24–34

Meditatio

"All these things the pagans seek."

The world of Jesus was not that different from our own. Taxes and financial pressures, inflation and recession, unemployment—all these realities mirror the insecurity and scarcity experienced by an oppressed people. Thus, Jesus' words about putting God, not wealth, first in our lives, would have hit his hearers as hard as they hit us today.

So how do we detach ourselves from the fear that drives us to anxiously strive for security in wealth? Jesus says that the pagans worry about security: what they will wear and eat, their jobs, how to pay the rent. Jesus is not saying we shouldn't have concern for these things, but that we shouldn't worry about them. He wants to free us from the weariness that comes from constant straining to achieve a goal by ourselves.

Disciples of Jesus, instead, are invited to trust. Put God and his will in first place, and everything else will be provided for. Of course, this means provided for according to God's will. That is why this invitation of Jesus requires so much trust. It is hard for us to believe that God has our true good at heart, that he will allow nothing to happen to us that will ultimately destroy us. But some things will happen that we don't like, that cut across our idea of what is in our best interest, that bring us down a peg. When these are received with trust, we discover that God uses them to bring about a new flourishing of life within us.

This is a secret I learned slowly since my early twenties. I had a major setback in my first years of religious life when I had a stroke. Life as I knew it was gone, with no assurance that I would recover. Mine is not a unique story. In some way or other all of us are put in this place. It is the only way we can learn the truth of this Gospel passage. Then, when we have deeply come to know God's faithful love in adversity, we can trust God with our lives and help others to do the same.

Oratio

Jesus, I hope you understand. Beneath my reluctance to trust you lies fear—fear of failure, fear of loneliness, fear of death. There is anger that you could have such control over my life, a refusal to give in to your loving embrace. So I squirm out of your arms again and again. I am sure you understand. You have a human heart. Most Sacred Heart of Jesus, purify my heart and help me to face my fears, that in facing them I may learn to trust you with my life.

Contemplatio

Teach me to trust you, my Lord and Savior.

Twelfth Sunday of Ordinary Time — Year A

∴ ⋯⋯⋯⋯ ∴

Lectio

Matthew 10:26–33

Meditatio

"So do not be afraid; you are worth more than many sparrows."

Today's reading from Matthew's Gospel is part of Jesus' "Mission Discourse" to his disciples as he prepares to send them out. The core of the message comprises words that echo throughout the Scriptures: "Do not be afraid." In fact, this message appears no fewer than three times in this short passage. And it is paired with tender images of God's loving care for his creation, a care that encompasses our whole being. "Even all the hairs of your head are counted." What a deep intimacy this conveys! It is like the kiss of the Father's love upon our lives.

Nonetheless, it is equally apparent that the Lord is not promising his disciples an easy passage, free of suffering or discord. On the contrary, Jesus acknowledges that some people will persecute them, and others will threaten their physical lives. Jesus does not promise a discipleship free of obstacles. He promises a discipleship that rests secure in the Father's loving embrace, even in the midst of adversity, need, and sorrow. In fact, Jesus promises that as long as we place our trust and our hope in him, we have nothing to fear, even from death itself.

In a world plagued by natural disasters, wars, and unfathomable forms of human cruelty, this message is on target. Things will not always go well for us, and we may not be able to comprehend the suffering around us. But we have a God who dwells with us, promising to remain with us always. We have a God who cries with us for a world torn by hatred and disease. And we have a God who continues to plant his seeds of hope and love *through us* for the sake of others. God is present to our world today. And as he sends us forth, he gives us the grace and the awesome responsibility to be the living proof of his presence and his love for all whom we meet.

Oratio

Jesus, as you send me forth today, I feel so small. Do you know whom you chose? Yes, you know every fiber of my being, every potential and every weakness. Help me to remember that the light and the love I am called to offer do not come from me, but from you. As I open my heart to you, I surrender to your loving embrace. I ask you to empty me of my fears so that you might fill me to the brim with all the utter fullness and beauty of God. As your love spills over me, may it become a wellspring of life and nourishment for all.

Contemplatio

Jesus assures us, "Do not be afraid. I am always with you."

Twelfth Sunday of Ordinary Time — Year B

∶⋯⋯⋯⋯∶

Lectio

Mark 4:35–41

Meditatio

"Why are you terrified?"

In times of crisis and suffering, has it ever seemed that Jesus is "asleep" in the boat of your life? Have you ever felt like screaming, "Jesus, don't you *care*?" as you sit watching a loved one die, or fumble for words to comfort a friend with a terminal illness, or struggle to push back a wave of panic after having been laid off from a job? If you have, then you know just how the disciples in today's Gospel passage feel— alone and helpless.

Although it seems that Jesus has abandoned them, this isn't the case at all. He is right there with them in the midst of their terrifying experience. The same is true for us. Jesus is right beside *us* in every pain, in every suffering, although we may rarely feel his presence. Precisely because he's with us, he asks, "Why are you terrified?"

Jesus wants our faith and trust! Even though it can be impossible to see while we're in the thick of a crisis, Jesus works through every time of suffering to bring about something wonderfully holy and good in our lives. It may be that he's strengthening us, purifying us, or increasing our desire for deeper union with him. However he works, Jesus is gradually transforming us through daily events into the persons he's created us to be. Jesus is Love, and his motive for allowing all that happens to us in life is love. We can trust that everything is only and always for our good.

At any moment, Jesus can command, "Quiet! Be still!" and the "storms" we're living through will cease just as surely as they did that day on the gale-tossed sea. Let's pray today for an increase of this faith. It can make all the difference in our lives.

Oratio

Jesus, you want me to be honest with you when I pray. I know you don't mind hearing my heart shout, "Don't you care?" Show me—in every difficult circumstance—that you do. Give me the faith and trust to believe that even when you seem to be asleep in my boat, just the opposite is true. I wait for you to calm my fears.

Contemplatio

Stay with me, Lord!

Twelfth Sunday of Ordinary Time — Year C

⁘· · · · · · · · · · · ·⁙

Lectio

Luke 9:18–24

Meditatio

". . . who do you say that I am?"

In the previous passage, Jesus has fed the multitudes with the five loaves and two fish (see Lk 9:10–17). It is easy to imagine the excitement of the event, as well as the exhaustion Jesus and the disciples probably felt afterward. In contrast, Luke tells us in today's passage: ". . . Jesus was praying in solitude, and [only] the disciples were with him. . . ." I am struck by the intimacy of this passage. Luke sets the stage for something important to be communicated.

In this context of solitude and prayer, Jesus wants to bring the disciples into deeper awareness of who he truly is for them. Curiously, Jesus first asks them what others think about him: "Who do the crowds say that I am?" Only after they have elaborated on the opinions circulating among the people does Jesus ask, "But who do *you* say that I am?"

On my nightstand I have a framed picture of Jesus who looks directly at me, with bright eyes smiling. A line on the bottom reads (in Spanish): "and you, who do *you* say that I am?" Like the disciples, I too have heard Jesus ask me this question. Like the disciples, I am sometimes uncomfortable answering. In coming to a deeper truth about who Jesus is, I am called to conversion in the way in which I follow him.

I confess that I know that Jesus is God, that he is the Christ, my Savior, and the Redeemer of the world. I also confess that I don't always act as one who believes this completely. Like the disciples, and the crowds who were fed, I want a Messiah who will be victoriously triumphant at all times. Yes, Jesus has won the victory . . . but he invites you and me to follow him as the Christ who lived, worked, suffered, was rejected, was put to death, and also rose again on the third day.

I hear Jesus inviting me, as he did Peter and the disciples, to deeper faith, a faith that accepts God's revelation of himself as he truly is.

Oratio

Jesus, I confess that you are the Christ, the Son of God. Lead me to deeper faith and trust in who you are. Help me to let go of my own expectations and open my heart to the revelation of who you are, at each moment. Jesus, give me courage to follow you in your paschal mystery, so that in daily dying and rising, I may open my life to you and let you live in me more and more. Amen.

Contemplatio

Lord Jesus, I believe that you are the Christ, the Son of the living God!

Monday of the Twelfth Week of Ordinary Time

⁘ · · · · · · · · · · · ⁘

Lectio

Matthew 7:1–5

Meditatio

> *"Stop judging, that you may not be judged."*

If a cartoonist illustrated the scene of a person with a beam in one eye removing a splinter from someone else's eye, we would doubtless find it humorous. Jesus' story presents an effective image about the nonsensical nature of negative judgment.

Our human minds ordinarily work by making judgments. For example, we are aware of personal experiences, and we understand and learn from them in order to reach a judgment or decision. This ordinary activity of our minds is not what the Gospel means when it commands us to "stop judging."

Instead, the judgment we are to avoid consists of the critical, harsh, disparaging sentences that we pass on other people. Since we cannot read others' minds and look into their hearts, we do not have enough information to make a sound judgment. But beyond this, our Christian love of neighbor and the respect we ought to have for each person preempt us from passing judgment. One day we will all be judged by God, and no one will be exempt. Saint Paul says: ". . . we shall all stand before the judgment seat of God" (Rom 14:10).

God is a good and just God. In a world filled with injustice, where innocent people are taken advantage of, we can be assured that God will give us an equitable, honest, loving hearing. He will act in justice because he is a good Father wishing the best for us, his children.

Oratio

With all the wrongdoing around me, Lord, I occasionally wonder if you will judge me gently, and if I will receive the justice that might have been denied me in this life. Then I remember your words in the Book of Isaiah, "For my thoughts are not your thoughts, nor are your ways my ways" (Is 55:8). Yes, I believe in your fairness, and I trust in you, my God!

Contemplatio

"Then let us no longer judge one another, but rather resolve never to put a stumbling block or hindrance in the way of a brother" (Rom 14:13).

Tuesday of the Twelfth Week
of Ordinary Time

⁖·············⁖

Lectio

Matthew 7:6, 12–14

Meditatio

> *"How narrow the gate . . . that leads to life.
> And those who find it are few."*

As I was making my daily commute one day, it hit me that I was actually living this Gospel. I was trying to catch the Staten Island Ferry, and the terminal workers were ready to close the doors to the crowd going into Manhattan. At a certain point, they must secure the area and make sure it is safe for the ferry to leave port. As the wide-open glass doors that separate the terminal (where I was) from the ferry (where I wanted to be) started to close, I and all the other late-comers broke into an all-out *run*. We made it just in time.

Once inside the safety zone, panting, I thought, "That was a real, visceral feeling of the narrow gate!" I was focused only on getting through that door. Nothing could distract me from my goal. Have you ever lived this? Hastening to make it just in time before the door closes . . . whether it's a ferryboat, a deadline, or a golden opportunity? All other worries take second place to the only thing that matters. That one all-consuming concern engages our entire being.

In these experiences, I think the Lord wants to actually show us how concerned he would like us to feel about the gate and the road that leads to life. Nothing else in the world can measure up to this in importance or urgency.

What path shall I take today? Will I take the way that gives life and shares it, that does unto others "whatever you would have them do to you"? Am I grateful to those who "hold the doors" and help me through life with their patience, kindness, or ability to overlook my foibles? How will I today hold the doors for others to enter this all-important way of life?

Oratio

Jesus, I get so distracted from the important things in life, sometimes not seeing the forest for the trees. You are my blessed Gate whom the Father sent to bring me to life. You have opened for me the way of holiness. Help me to find the way you would like me to walk today. Travel with me and help me to open the gate to others.

Contemplatio

"Do to others whatever you would have them do to you."

Wednesday of the Twelfth Week of Ordinary Time

∴ · · · · · · · · · · · ∴

Lectio

Matthew 7:15–20

Meditatio

"So by their fruits you will know them."

Jesus is counseling the disciples to avoid being naive. He wants followers who are simple, that is, childlike in their simplicity—uncomplicated, unsophisticated, but wise, aware, and astute. We should know our faith well enough to realize when we are being fed an untruth and familiar enough with Christ's life to recognize a charlatan. Some people use religion for various types of gain: money, pleasure, honor. Occasionally someone will use religion as a front for evil purposes: to steal, to harass, to exploit. Jesus uses the example of the wolf in sheep's clothing, possibly a popular metaphor of his day, to help us picture the danger. I immediately think of the stuffed animal—a wolf with a removable sheepskin—that sat for many years in my parents' living room. Their grandchildren loved to play with it. Real-life versions aren't as easily identified. Whom exactly is Jesus cautioning against? Perhaps certain people are infiltrating his group of followers with bad intentions. Perhaps he is pointing out the deceptions all too common in every society.

Jesus continues his advice by turning our attention from the malicious to the misleading. How often have we opened a beautiful piece of fruit to find it rotten inside? A good tree would not have borne this fruit. However, the tree must have looked healthy, or the harvesters would have passed it by. Jesus is telling us to avoid being hypocritical. To mean what we say, yes or no. To not appear pious while entertaining evil thoughts. To not pass ourselves off as tough, crass, or arrogant while thinking of ourselves as holy souls. To be who we say we are: let baptism show. It is not just a metaphor that dead wood will be cut down and thrown into the fire. "By their fruits you will know them." Jesus repeats this twice, to open and close this teaching, in order to impress its importance on us. Jesus wants us to be genuine and sincere.

Oratio

Dear Lord, help us to be aware that we always have the choice of producing good fruit or of wasting our great gifts. Let our fruit be sweet and nourishing for all whom we encounter. Let our demeanor always give us away as your followers. Let there never be any question about who we are. May our baptism color every aspect of our life so that seeing us, others may see you, the true Light of the World.

Contemplatio

"You can tell a tree by its fruit."

Thursday of the Twelfth Week of Ordinary Time

∴ · · · · · · · · · · · · ∴

Lectio

Matthew 7:21–29

Meditatio

"I never knew you."

I've often heard comments like these: "Can you pray for me? God will listen to your prayers, Sister, since you have done so many things for him." "I don't know if I'll go to heaven, I haven't done for God what you have done." Somehow the message of this Gospel passage has been lost.

In parishes and Catholic schools people are encouraged to participate, to belong, to contribute, to help out and give in countless ways. If you're like me, you could think the goal is to arrive at the gates of heaven with a long list of things we've done for people, mission, and the Church.

The list of what people on the last day will say they have done in Jesus' name is the same list mentioned in Luke's Gospel (10:17–20) when the seventy-two disciples return exultant to Jesus: "Lord, it was so great! Even the devils were subject to us in your name!" And Jesus responds: "I saw Satan fall from the sky. But don't rejoice over these things. Rejoice that your names are written in heaven." Rejoice over a complete *gift*. Forget about those other things that seem so great, because they accumulate nothing for you. You can't stack them up or add them up to buy anything.

Today's Gospel concludes the Sermon on the Mount. Nowhere in the sermon does Jesus ask his followers to do any showy things. Instead he asks for poverty of spirit and gentleness, prayer and fasting done in secret, forgiveness and the gift of self, living by the Golden Rule, and rejecting money as one's master. It would be quite a surprise for someone who did all kinds of good things yet neglected these weightier matters of the Father's will to hear from Jesus, "I never asked you to do these things. You have tried to do *my* job. You missed the point that I did all these mighty acts in the humiliating poverty of the cross. But you haven't done what I asked *you* to do. So I have not truly *been known by you*."

Oratio

Lord, I remember the more poetic parts of the Sermon on the Mount: flowers of the field, birds of the air, gentle spirits, and such. They are consoling, but I hardly have taken them as a program of life. Give me the grace to read the Scriptures in relationship with you. Help me listen to what *you* want of me this day, now.

Contemplatio

What do you ask of me, Lord, today?

Friday of the Twelfth Week
of Ordinary Time

⁘············⁘

Lectio

Matthew 8:1–4

Meditatio

> *"Lord, if you wish, you can make me clean."*

I open the sacred text today and step into it, knowing that this story of salvation is also my story. It's easy to immediately get caught up in today's reading. I begin by watching Jesus as he comes down the mountain. I join the ranks of the great crowds following him, and keep my eyes and heart open.

An outcast approaches Jesus—a leper. The crowd draws back in fear of the disease. I hear the man with leprosy simply say "if you wish, you can. . . ." It would be such an ordinary request if it weren't a healing that he wanted! For Jesus though, it is a simple matter. "I will do it," and it's done, just like that. The leper is cured immediately, so great is Jesus' power to heal.

I dwell on the leper's words, "Lord, if you wish, you can make me clean." This phrase is so powerful, packed with so much confidence. "If you wish" presupposes that the one making the request believes that the Lord does care, does really desire one's good. In this case, it is to be made clean.

We have so many things to be cleansed of! They could be outright sin, unhelpful attitudes, or a myriad of other possible burdens.

How many times have I asked the Teacher to cleanse me, desiring renewed wholeness through the sacrament of Reconciliation! I have requested this in words similar to the leper's, desiring pardon or asking for any needed healing of body, mind, or spirit.

Yes, Lord, you can make me clean. The leper in the Gospel story has walked away, and I stand there in his place, looking up expectantly. I know that you can do this. I trust that you want to do this. I just need the faith today to see how you are working in my life, making me clean. No one desires my good as much as you do.

Oratio

Lord, thank you for your love for me. No one is as much on my side as you are. You keep on working on me, consistently, fashioning me into a true disciple who looks to you to teach me through everything that happens. I trust that you will help me keep my heart open to you so you can continually mold me in your divine image. In all the circumstances of my life, you are with me. Thank you for walking with me.

Contemplatio

I know that the Lord desires my good. I delight in his care.

Saturday of the Twelfth Week
of Ordinary Time

⁝············⁝

Lectio

Matthew 8:5–17

Meditatio

". . . subject to authority . . ."

My respects, Sir. I don't know what possessed me, a Gentile, to come to you, a Jew, for a favor. It should be the other way around. Desperation, I suppose. It drives us all to do the unthinkable. My serving boy is racked with pain. I wish you'd. . . .

Come? No, I don't want to inconvenience you. Look at this mass of humanity that you're inexplicably devoted to. They sense it. They swarm around you, pressing for their miracles. So do I, confound it. The worst part is, I'm the outsider, less deserving of your attention than they are. So just give the order, and I'll melt back into the scenery.

The order. Rome invented law and order, or so it would have us think. It's practiced on us enough. Now, I may not be a Roman myself, but I've picked up a thing or two in this business. You and I, Sir—we know how it works. We say "Jump!" and everybody asks, "How high?"

No doubt your authority's different. Your power certainly is, and in my experience those two go together. I don't claim to understand you, but I've heard of your power, and it's leagues ahead of mine. What must your authority be? If my rank can command obedience, my guess is yours can do even more. "Only say the word . . . ."

Someday the community that follows you, clothed with your power and authority, will teach, unite, challenge, heal, forgive, and bear scarring from this world's ills—like you. Maybe then we'll have a chance to learn what real power and justice are. What promise, what hope! It could change the world.

For now, though, just heal my boy . . . Lord.

Oratio

Amazing. An outsider's unvarnished faith startled even you, Jesus. Just when I think I have salvation—and you—figured out, people upend it all. Thank you for reminding me that the last in my estimation will be the first in yours, and that faith as the work of the Spirit blows where it will, even "from the east and the west."

Through our faith your death and resurrection give us life. The Eucharist, sign of faith in the power of this paschal mystery, will one day heal us forever. That's because faith is relationship, mystery: you accept us where we are and take us where we can't imagine. Ready me by the obedience of my faith, such as it is. "Only say the word."

Contemplatio

Only say the word, and I will be healed.

Thirteenth Sunday of Ordinary Time—
Year A

⁘ · · · · · · · · · · · · ⁘

Lectio

Matthew 10:37–42

Meditatio

". . . worthy of me . . ."

"Worthy" is a loaded word. We echo the centurion's words at every Mass: "Lord, I am not worthy. . . ." In the parables of the prodigal son and the publican, both declare their unworthiness, and both are raised up to us as examples of a correct attitude. Yet here is Jesus boldly requiring the next-to-impossible lest we be found *not* worthy of him.

Love Jesus more than father, mother, son, or daughter? Family bonds are deep and instinctual. He expects more? Yes, he does. It was a shocking demand in first-century Palestine, and if we really listen to today's Gospel, it should be just as shocking to us, too.

What does Jesus mean when he talks about being "worthy" of him? But for his grace, all of our efforts at virtue and the spiritual life would be futile. So why does he speak in this way to his disciples and to us? His next words raise the bar even higher (if that's even possible!), ". . . whoever does not take up his cross and follow after me is not worthy of me." In Matthew's Gospel, the first prediction of the Passion comes much later after today's selection (in chapter 16), so what would the disciples have made of these words about carrying one's cross? More important, what do I make of these words? I know the end of the story (resurrection and salvation), but does that make it any easier for me?

I claim to follow Jesus, and I want to follow Jesus, but in my concrete actions what do I really choose to do? To be worthy of him, Jesus is asking us to enter into his pattern of self-giving love that takes its cue first and foremost from God. Jesus issues both an invitation and a command. *Follow me, live in me, love in the manner that I love.*

Am I up to this challenge?

Oratio

Lord, both you and I know I am not worthy of you. Despite my best efforts, I fall short of your example. In practice I prefer my agenda to yours.

But knowing all this ahead of time, you still call me to follow you. Jesus, I want to be worthy of you. I want to honor your trust and your dreams for me. Say but the word, Lord, and in this moment my soul will find the healing and strength to start afresh, to place you at the center of my life and my choices.

Contemplatio

Follow me, live in me, love in the manner that I love.

Thirteenth Sunday of Ordinary Time
—Year B

❖ · · · · · · · · · · · · ❖

Lectio

Mark 5:21–43

Meditatio

"Jesus, aware at once that power had gone out from him . . ."

Humans react instinctively in certain situations. Some things are hard-wired into us. If you are walking through uncut grass and notice something long and skinny rustling at your feet, chances are you'll jump back five feet before you realize that it was only a stick and not a snake. Survival mode takes over before we even have a chance to form a rational thought or make a careful analysis.

I like to think of this cure of the woman with the hemorrhage as a moment when Jesus' human nature kicks in, and he acts before he has time to think about it. Power goes out of him first, and a split second later he is aware of it. Instinctively he heals this woman.

Jesus is God, and his impulsive desire for the wholeness and integrity of this woman takes on a dimension that we mere mortals cannot attain. He can heal by willing it to be so. We cannot. But all the same, I wonder whether this reaction of Jesus gives us a glimpse of how our human nature is meant to be sensitive to the needs of others. Clearly Jesus' gut-level reactions are not turned in upon his health and well-being only—they are opened up to embrace the other. Is it not a result of original sin that we see the other as a potential threat . . . that we can talk about looking out for number one at the expense of others?

Virtue is defined as the habit of doing good. It means that one's desires are so in balance that choosing what is right, good, and uplifting comes naturally to a person. That is a picture of virtue at an instinctual level, one that I want to aspire to within the limits of my human nature.

Oratio

Lord, I live in a world where the mind, the heart, and bodily instincts are out of sync. The fabric of our nature's original integrity is torn and we are bleeding. Lord, heal me, heal us. Bring us back into harmony with ourselves and with one another, so that our instinctual choices include the well-being of those around us.

Contemplatio

Go in peace—go in wholeness.

Thirteenth Sunday of Ordinary Time
—Year C

⁘ · · · · · · · · · · · · ⁘

Lectio

Luke 9:51–62

Meditatio

> ". . . the Son of Man has nowhere to rest his head."

Jesus is on a journey to Jerusalem, and it seems that his disciples have to hurry to keep up with him! Luke highlights this journey, because it is Jesus' last. It will end in his passion, death, and resurrection. As the group moves along, a man comes up to Jesus and declares that he wants to follow him, "wherever you go." And Jesus answers that nature provides a place for the animals and the birds, but he, the Son of Man, "has nowhere to rest his head."

Jesus' words point out to me the cost of being his disciple. He wanted that enthusiastic would-be follower to know that discipleship is not an easy road. It is a relationship, and it comes with a cost. Comfort is the first thing one loses in a life on the road, spreading the Good News.

Yet how poignant are these words of Jesus! They put me face to face with a suffering that is so universal, shared by countless numbers of my fellow humans: homelessness. I want to stop and clear my mind of all the possible reasons for this, and just contemplate how a person who has no home feels at night. When I turn out the lights at night and go to rest, I may not think of how many people are just as tired as I, probably even more so. Yet, like the Savior before them, they have no place to rest their heads. Jesus wants them to be comforted, to know that he has walked this road, too, and that he has shared all our sufferings just as he has redeemed us from the burden of all our sins.

As Jesus' disciple, am I ready to put my comfort on the line, to join the band that walks with him, even at the cost of some sacrifice?

Oratio

Good Savior, help me to look beyond the ho-hum reality of my life, to see what waits "out there" for my dedication. Help me to see clearly that I will only find myself when I go out of myself to be a brother or sister to those less fortunate. Whether I do little or much isn't the point here: imitating your compassion and goodness is. I want to belong to your family, Jesus, and I realize that if I take you in, all the people you love come with you. They are part of the deal. That's okay. You can give me love and generosity as I need them. Just help me get started, Jesus. Help me get started . . .

Contemplatio

Help me get started—the world is waiting.

Monday of the Thirteenth Week
of Ordinary Time

⁝ · · · · · · · · · · · · ⁞

Lectio

Matthew 8:18–22

Meditatio

> *"Teacher, I will follow you wherever you go."*

To the well-meaning scribe and potential disciple who makes this magnanimous offer to Jesus, he offers a strange response: "Foxes have dens and birds of the sky have nests, but the Son of Man has nowhere to rest his head." Some interpret this mainly as an invitation to poverty as lived by the Master. I find it, however, still to be an intriguing response.

Note the scribe's word: *wherever*, and Jesus' word: *nowhere*. The scribe sees discipleship as being about location, perhaps even geographical location. He'll go anywhere to follow Jesus. But Jesus talks about "nowhere." Dens and nests for foxes and birds are their home bases from which they venture forth. Perhaps Jesus is saying it's not about location, nor doing dazzling things to public acclaim.

The scribe's *locus*, however, may be deeper than geography. Perhaps Jesus is addressing the *I* in the sentence. "I will follow you," the scribe glibly announces. I will do it. I will accomplish it on my own power because I want to do it. I am bestowing something on you, Lord, that you should be grateful for: myself. To that Jesus says, "I have no home base. I don't have a strategy or master plan creating around me a monument to myself. I don't have and can't offer anyone else the security of success, or accomplishment of any kind. In fact, I came for just the opposite: complete inner poverty and obedience to the Father. I will be emptied out in failure on the cross and buried in the tomb. Anyone who follows me must expect the same. It's about what God desires and his glory."

I've had to learn this lesson of the *nowhere* of the Master again and again. Unexpected illness or accident, failure in apostolic work, misunderstanding . . . my list is not so different from yours. The *nowhere* is God's way of deepening our life, of emptying us of ourselves, of making room for him and for our deepest happiness.

Oratio

Jesus, empty me of myself, of my self-assured discipleship that sets me up for spiritual superficiality. May I be given the grace to follow you *nowhere*, for without you I can accomplish nothing good, nothing of value, nothing of lasting merit. I rejoice to see my weakness, because if I turn to you in my weakness you will carry me in your strength where I could never go on my own.

Contemplatio

Teacher, may I follow you in your complete inner obedience to the Father.

Tuesday of the Thirteenth Week
of Ordinary Time

✦ · · · · · · · · · · · ✦

Lectio

Matthew 8:23–27

Meditatio

"Lord, save us!"

Today's Gospel paints a dramatic picture for us. Jesus and his disciples are sailing on the sea when suddenly a violent storm breaks out. The rough sea tosses the boat as waves crash over it and fill it with water. We can imagine the power of this storm. The disciples are terrified, afraid for their lives. When they turn to Jesus, however, he is sound asleep! How can he sleep at a time like this? Perhaps he is very tired. But perhaps it is because Jesus is not afraid. His dialogue with the frightened disciples indicates this may be the case, for he asks: "Why are you terrified, O you of little faith?" The disciples are afraid because they don't have much faith. Jesus, instead, is *not* afraid because he trusts his Father.

We too want to trust God in a similar way as we encounter storms in life. We know that faith is not a feeling, but a deep belief in all that God has revealed. Our deep beliefs give us the courage to be faithful and to continue on in all of the circumstances of our daily life. These beliefs lead us to trust in God's merciful and powerful love for us.

Just as Jesus intervenes in the storm in today's Gospel, he also intervenes in our storms and in all that challenges us. Sometimes he does this in a dramatic way and at other times he walks along with us, listens to us, encourages us, strengthens us, and gives us the graces we need to be faithful to our commitments and choices. Jesus also brings unimaginable good out of whatever challenges and sufferings we encounter and endure.

In the midst of the storm, the disciples turn to Jesus, "Lord, save us! We are perishing!" This is the key: believing and trusting. We can confidently turn to Jesus for help, for he is faithful.

Oratio

Jesus, what an example you give me! Your trust in your Father gave you courage and kept you calm. How I want this! It would help me to reflect more often on your goodness, mercy, and unconditional love for me. If I would remember that you never abandon me and are able to bring good out of every circumstance, I would learn to trust you more. Please help me, Jesus. Deepen these beliefs in my heart. Obtain for me the gifts of a deeper faith and trust. During the day, remind me to turn to you in all of my needs.

Contemplatio

I place my trust in your saving help.

Wednesday of the Thirteenth Week
of Ordinary Time

∴···········∴

Lectio

Matthew 8:28–34

Meditatio

> "*. . . they begged him to leave their district.*"

If you knew that Jesus was coming to your town, would you rush out to see him? Or would you instead beg him to go away? In today's Gospel, the Gadarenes want Jesus to leave their town. He has cured two demoniacs, and the demons rush into a herd of swine and drive them off a cliff. Do the townspeople fear that Jesus wants to destroy them? Do they look on him as some kind of magician who might trick them into something they don't want to do? Or do they just not want to be bothered with changing the routine of their life?

We don't know the answers to these questions and can only speculate about them. The incident with the swine may seem strange to us. But for Matthew's Jewish audience, pigs were unclean animals. They would have laughed at the story of the pigs drowning. The pigs' demise wouldn't have bothered them any more than exterminating rats bothers us today. In the context in which Matthew sets this story, his focus is on showing the power of Jesus at work in his mighty deeds.

In yesterday's Gospel he calmed the storm, and in tomorrow's we will see him healing the paralyzed man and forgiving sins. Yesterday, the disciples were amazed at Jesus' power, and tomorrow, some will be blind to Jesus' authority and accuse him of blasphemy. But today the townspeople just want to get rid of Jesus. They don't know what to make of him, so they want him to just go away.

What about me? Do I want Jesus to go away? Or do I really want to follow him, to be his disciple, no matter what it costs? Jesus warned us that following him means taking up our cross every day. It might be hard right now. But if I imagine myself at the end of my life, looking back on how I lived it, I know that my only choice is Jesus.

Oratio

Jesus, I want to invite you into my life. When you come to me, I want to rush out to meet you and get right out in front where I can stretch out my hand and touch you. Don't let my fears hold me back. You may lead me by new and different roads, but I trust you'll always walk by my side. Together we can do amazing things.

Contemplatio

Stay with me, Lord.

Thursday of the Thirteenth Week of Ordinary Time

∴ · · · · · · · · · · · · ∴

Lectio

Matthew 9:1–8

Meditatio

"Courage, child, your sins are forgiven."

This event, telescoped as it is in a rather breathless style, leaves me stunned at the raw human interchange between the quick judgments of the scribes and Jesus' rapid response. He works this cure to prove his authority to forgive sin on earth. Jesus is moved with compassion for this paralyzed man and ready to lead him to a new life with his healing. But the Lord is sidetracked by the rash judgment of the scribes. How disappointed Jesus must have felt to be interrupted by such thoughts, which attack his mission at its foundations. The people, and this unfortunate paralyzed man, need to be reassured that the kingdom of God has come even for them.

As I ponder the word of God with reverence, I see how intent Jesus is on fulfilling his mission to bring the Good News of forgiveness, healing, and a new creation! He offers this to every person, not just the religious elite. The hope for healing will need only faith to keep it alive, not wealth, social position, or learning.

Forgiveness is what Jesus always does first. For most of us it is the most difficult of Jesus' teachings to follow, and the hallmark of every person's faith. Jesus' words to this paralytic are meant for me, too. Strengthened by his grace, I want go one step farther, bringing forgiveness into all my relationships with Jesus' same delicacy and love.

I will count on Jesus' fidelity today and every day, knowing that Jesus left his earthly life, his miracles, his death, and his forgiveness to me as my own down payment on the kingdom of God.

Oratio

Jesus, as I move along the road of earthly existence with great effort and fatigue, and often with pain and suffering, you come walking into my life. You bring your Good News of the kingdom of God, a kingdom to which you invite us all with your forgiveness and love. I place my hand in yours, taking heart from your grace and forgiveness. Lead me home, Lord Jesus. Lead me home.

Contemplatio

"Courage . . ."

Friday of the Thirteenth Week
of Ordinary Time

⁘ · · · · · · · · · · · ⁘

Lectio

Matthew 9:9–13

Meditatio

"As Jesus passed by . . ."

How do we know Jesus is passing by? In other words, how do we know if a project is inspired by the Lord? How do we know if the Spirit is urging us to do something? How do we know if a movement in our hearts is revealing something God wills?

We need to ponder these questions every day. Why? Because this Gospel shows us the breathtaking results of noticing Jesus pass by. While Matthew is in the midst of his daily activity, he sees Jesus and hears him speak to him. He gets up and does what Jesus asks. Then he invites Jesus to a meal in his home with all his friends.

Initially, the key moment is in the *noticing.* How do we see him? How do we hear him? How can we follow when we've neither seen him pass by nor heard his voice? It was much easier for Matthew. He couldn't miss Jesus standing right in front of him. But could it be that Jesus was here only for the few people he met in Palestine during his earthly life? No. He promised us his Spirit, who would remind us of Jesus and all his words after he had returned to the Father. So how do we notice the Spirit? It's not as difficult or elusive as one might think.

The images of wind and fire herald the Spirit's coming. It's easy to notice strong winds and burning flames. The wind and flame of the Spirit's presence are felt in the movements of our heart: movements toward God, faith, love, and a sense of God's love for us. We also learn to distinguish movements in our heart away from God, feelings of being abandoned by God, of desolation, hopelessness, and self-centeredness. Sensitivity to these movements helps us to notice "Jesus passing by." Often during the day, therefore, we might want to ask: what is happening in my heart? To what are my thoughts leading? To what actions am I being drawn? When I think of them, do I feel drawn to God, or away from him?

Oratio

Jesus, you pass by me countless times each day, beckoning me to let you into my life. When my thoughts about myself and others are thoughts of mercy, then I know you are passing by. When I am inflamed with trust and love, you are passing by. When I have a sense of forgiveness and kindness, you are passing by. When I am confused in the darkness, pass by and call me into the light. I will follow wherever you lead.

Contemplatio

Jesus, when you pass by, call me by name.

Saturday of the Thirteenth Week of Ordinary Time

∴· · · · · · · · · · · ·∴

Lectio

Matthew 9:14–17

Meditatio

> *"The days will come when the bridegroom*
> *is taken away from them, and then they will fast."*

So—do we feast or do we fast? Is the Bridegroom present or absent?

I think the answer is that typical Catholic response: Not *either . . . or,* but *both . . . and.*

The Bridegroom is absent from our gaze but present in our hearts. We certainly can feast on these summer days, but it wouldn't hurt to do a little fasting as well—acknowledging our longing for the full coming of the kingdom.

Fasting can have many purposes. Some are pragmatic, such as improved health or greater self-discipline. In the long run it's more beneficial to fast out of love for the Lord and offer it up with the desire that God will bless others.

Fasting can take various forms. For example, when vacationing with family or friends, I may have to renounce some of my preferences out of consideration for those of others. Besides doing this for love of my companions, I can add the intention of love for God.

Fasting can also take the form of *delayed gratification*. Instead of popping that chocolate into my mouth here and now, I can wait a few minutes. Or if lunch will be ready in half an hour, I can wait until the established time rather than nibble beforehand. We live in an era when so much is available instantaneously that it has become harder to wait for anything. (Witness our fidgets while waiting for a computer program to load!) It's good to remember how to wait.

Our *intention* is the most important thing. We do it not primarily for self, but for the Lord.

So in these summer days we both feast and fast.

Oratio

Lord Jesus, you, the Bridegroom, are still with us. Teach me how to live a balanced life—to know when to feast and how to fast. When I feast, I want to acknowledge your goodness in my heart and on my lips, enjoying what your bounty has provided. But on some days I'll want to express my love and gratitude through some little sacrifice, just as I might make a sacrifice to show my love for a family member or friend. I ask you to bless my good intentions and accept these little gifts that I offer from my heart. Amen.

Contemplatio

Not *either . . . or*, but *both . . . and*.

Fourteenth Sunday of Ordinary Time
—Year A

❖ · · · · · · · · · · · · ❖

Lectio

Matthew 11:25–30

Meditatio

"Come to me . . ."

In the Catholic hospital where I received cancer treatment, I would often visit the quiet chapel with its beautiful stained glass windows that let colored light play on the walls. I noticed that other people, too, came into the chapel to pay brief visits to Jesus in the Blessed Sacrament. Christ seems to be inviting each of us with the words in today's Gospel: "Come to me, all you who labor and are burdened, and I will give you rest."

This passage is one of many consoling sections in Scripture where we meet the compassionate, merciful, loving face of the Father revealed through his Son, Jesus Christ. In this Gospel, Jesus seems to be debunking the heavy burdens that the scribes unnecessarily added to the law. Instead, Christ explains that his "yoke," that is, obedience to his teachings, is easier and lighter. His invitation, "Come to me . . . and you will find rest" is addressed to all peoples throughout time.

He goes even further by appealing to us to take up his yoke and to follow his example, so as to walk steadily and joyfully on our Christian journey. Whatever our labors and burdens, Christ wants us to share them with him. His goodness draws our hearts to him. We need not fear. He will carry our tiredness, sufferings—difficulties of all sorts—and will give us rest.

At the beginning of today's Gospel, Jesus addresses the Father in words of praise and gratitude. In his ecstatic prayer, Jesus is happy that the humble of this world are receptive to God's word.

Praise and *confidence* are powerful messages to take from today's reading: *praise* for all that the Lord does in us and for us, and full *confidence* in the love, meekness, and humility of Jesus, who calls us to himself and wishes to share our heavy load.

Oratio

Jesus, keep inviting me to turn to you. I trust that you will always share my "yoke" and will offer me your precious rest. I praise and thank you! Keep inviting those also who have not yet heard your invitation and feel they have nowhere to place their burdens.

Contemplatio

Let me come to you and unburden my heart.

Fourteenth Sunday of Ordinary Time
—Year B

∴ · · · · · · · · · · · ∴

Lectio

Mark 6:1–6

Meditatio

> *"He was amazed at their lack of faith."*

The synagogue is abuzz—both the men's and women's sections. As the murmuring grows louder, the man who is commenting on the Scriptures pauses. Hardly anyone notices—so absorbed are they in their own conversations:

"Why is *he* trying to teach *us*?"

"He's just the carpenter—Mary's son."

"James and Joses are his brothers."

"So are Judas and Simon."

Gesturing toward the women's section, one of the men adds, "And aren't his sisters here with us?"

Gradually the townsfolk begin to realize that Jesus has stopped speaking and is staring at them. They quiet down.

"The only place a prophet isn't given recognition," Jesus observes, "is in his own hometown and among his own relatives."

Mark doesn't relate what happened next—only that a few sick people presented themselves to Jesus and he healed them.

He also states that Jesus was amazed at the lack of faith he found in his native Nazareth. It seems that few people believed in Jesus beyond his mother and perhaps his aunt, mother of James and Joses, who would one day witness his crucifixion from afar.

Jesus may have wondered: Why are their minds closed? Are prophets expected to emerge from nowhere with no human origins?

In any case, his hands were tied by the townspeople's lack of faith.

God created us as free beings and doesn't force us to believe. But, as Saint Augustine observed, he who created us without our consent won't save us without our consent. We have to do our part.

Oratio

My God and Father, at times I'm baffled by the mystery of human freedom. You wanted us to resemble you, so you gave us intelligence and free will. Yet, you knew we would use them wrongly or poorly. How often we fail or waver in believing, in trusting, in doing good! Through Jesus, your Son, I ask the grace to firmly believe and trust in you and to live as Jesus' devoted disciple.

Contemplatio

Lord, increase my faith!

Fourteenth Sunday of Ordinary Time
—Year C

⁜· · · · · · · · · · · ·⁜

Lectio

Luke 10:1–12, 17–20

Meditatio

"Peace to this household."

This Gospel has a sense of urgency. Jesus doesn't waste words. He has a mission to entrust to these seventy-two disciples, and he wants them to be crystal clear about it.

In saying he is sending them "like lambs among wolves" he probably gets their attention quickly enough. He is not sending them on a grand adventure, a tour, or vacation, not even a pilgrimage. To be like lambs among wolves is to be completely vulnerable to attack, even to destruction. Are they to go armed so as to defend themselves? Not only does Jesus mention no arms, but he also reduces their possessions to the minimum—"no money bag, no sack, no sandals." They are to "greet no one along the way." Jesus is determined that his disciples will not be distracted from the mission he is entrusting to them. They are to enter into it with full focus and exclusive attention, undistracted by any of the compelling voices that might divert them from their goal.

Why does he have to drive his point home so strongly? These disciples do not have the slightest fraction of the distractions we have today. Is it really so hard for them to focus, too? Is our common human nature so vulnerable just by itself, without taking into account external circumstances? I know that it takes the Lord a long time to get my attention. And it's usually not even bad things that distract me. A thousand good things can make me trip—a favor here, a duty there, something to put away, something to write down. . . . Jesus uses rather extreme language to get his disciples to focus and concentrate on essentials.

What is the essential message he wants them to communicate? "Peace to this household." This is the message they must deliver with an urgency that could brook no delay. But to deliver the message effectively, they first have to receive it themselves. If I could lay everything else aside and receive Jesus' message of peace, would I lack anything else?

Oratio

Lord, help me to accept my utter vulnerability as a gift, a gift intended by you to open me up to your peace. To be a lamb among wolves need not bring fear—it can bring freedom. I have nothing, so I have nothing to lose! Only you can give me that true peace to which genuine freedom is the companion. Everything that leads me away from you is only distraction and illusion. Help me to focus my attention so I may keep my eyes on you, Lord.

Contemplatio

Your peace, Lord, I desire.

Monday of the Fourteenth Week
of Ordinary Time

∴ · · · · · · · · · · · ∴

Lectio

Matthew 9:18–26

Meditatio

"The girl is not dead but sleeping."

Today's Gospel follows upon the words of Jesus: "No one patches an old cloak with a piece of unshrunken cloth. . . . People do not put new wine into old wineskins. . . . Rather pour new wine into fresh wineskins" (Mt 9:16–17).

Four times in today's Gospel, the new wine bursts out of the old skins to bestow life and joy. First the official, a grieving father, approaches this unorthodox rabbi. The Greek word used to denote his status means that he was a principal official, a representative of the ideal Jew, an establisher of order in the synagogue. Yet he doesn't seem to care that he will be associated with this man whom the Pharisees are already considering with caution.

Second, Jesus gets up immediately to go with the ruler to see his daughter who has died, even though touching a dead person would make Jesus unclean for seven days and require a ritual of purification.

Third, Jesus allows himself to be touched by a woman who has been rendered unclean for twelve years due to her hemorrhaging. Surely she knows the position she was putting Jesus in by touching the hem of his garment. Jesus rewards her bold faith with the vision of his face and the assurance of his words that her faith has healed her.

Fourth, when Jesus arrives at the ruler's house, he tells the wailing women and flute players to go away because the girl is not dead. The father trusts Jesus' word and puts them out of the room. Jesus takes the girl by the hand and raises her. Ultimately this is the boldest and most joyous proclamation of all. Death has been destroyed by the new wine, by Jesus, the Son of God and Savior of the world.

Nothing can stand in the way of Jesus' love. He pours out on humanity and each human soul the wine of his blood, which was pressed on the winepress of the cross to destroy sin and death forever.

Oratio

Lord, every time I receive your body and blood in the Eucharist, I too am touching the hem of your garment. You are coming to my house; you are raising what is dead in me to life. Give me the vision of your face, the joy of the official as he received his daughter back into his arms alive. Don't let me become callous to your majesty or bored with the gift of your love.

Contemplatio

O Lord, I am not worthy to receive you.

Tuesday of the Fourteenth Week of Ordinary Time

:·············:

Lectio

Matthew 9:32–38

Meditatio

> *". . . his heart was moved with pity for them . . ."*

Jesus has healed a few other people of different infirmities prior to healing the mute person, also described as a "demoniac." Immediately after Jesus heals him, the ordinary people proclaim "Nothing like this has ever been seen in Israel." The Pharisees, instead, claim that Jesus commands devils to leave their victims not by the power of God, but by the power of the devil.

The people in the crowd marvel over the fact that neither they nor their ancestors had ever seen anything like this. In other words, they are saying that what Jesus is doing is even greater than the marvels the Lord had done through Moses, who led the Israelites out of Egypt. But then the Pharisees say that Jesus' power comes from the devil! What a letdown! What dejection this must have caused in the crowd. These poor people—no wonder the Lord has pity on them.

Rather, all of these miracles are a direct sign that Jesus is the Messiah—that he is the one God promised to send: "A prophet like me will the LORD, your God, raise up for you from among your own kinsmen; to him you shall listen" (Dt 18:15). Jesus himself tells John's followers something similar when they come to ask Jesus if he is the Messiah (see Mt 11:2–6).

The truth is that we ourselves may at times attribute God's gifts to other sources, such as luck or coincidence. We might even take away the joy of others when they bask in the marvels God has done for them. I think that Jesus' heart "was moved with pity for them" when he saw the dejection that the crowds must have felt. He recognizes their need, my need, for a shepherd—someone who guides us to true life, God's life. That Shepherd always takes delight in those he shepherds.

Oratio

Jesus, I believe that you healed and continue to heal because you are God—the Messiah. But I don't always recognize that all I am blessed with comes from God. Sometimes I allow myself to believe that I am gifted and blessed for other reasons. This attitude creates a distance between you and me. Help me to allow myself to be guided by you, my Shepherd. By allowing you to shepherd me, I will be healed and will become a healing presence for others. Then I may be among the laborers privileged to have been chosen by your father to work in his harvest. Amen.

Contemplatio

Jesus, my shepherd, you have truly blessed me.

Wednesday of the Fourteenth Week
of Ordinary Time

∶············∶

Lectio

Matthew 10:1–7

Meditatio

"Jesus sent out these twelve. . . ."

They are twelve—the group of disciples Jesus is about to send out to proclaim the dawn of the kingdom. As a good teacher, the Divine Master has first *shown* them how to preach, heal, and expel unclean spirits (see Mt 9:35). Now he is sending them out on their own to do the same.

Jesus tells the apostles that they are to prepare the people for his coming visit. But isn't it likely that this hands-on experience is also intended to prepare these men for their future mission?

When the Twelve begin preaching after Pentecost, how different their focus will be! During Jesus' earthly lifetime, they preached the *nearness of the kingdom* to "the lost sheep of the house of Israel." After Pentecost they will preach the *death and resurrection of Jesus* to Israel first, and later to everyone. The message is to be carried to the ends of the earth.

As we know, universality is the very meaning of being Catholic. All people are invited to belong to the Church.

As the apostles went out to bring that invitation to everyone they met, we too can do the same. We can bring it in our own way to the people in our personal world who have fallen away or are searching for God.

Our method probably won't involve preaching or teaching, but rather witnessing. As Pope Paul VI wrote, people in our times are more influenced by witnesses than by teachers, and if they do pay attention to teachers, it's because they're witnesses. If we sincerely live our faith, others will be drawn to the Church in God's good time. He's relying on our cooperation, as he relied on the preaching of the apostles.

Oratio

Holy Spirit, as you have guided Jesus' disciples down through the ages, please guide me. I want to live up to the graces of Baptism and Confirmation, witnessing to Jesus among my friends, relatives, coworkers, and acquaintances. Please help me to know at the right moment what to do and what to say. Jesus taught that the Church is called to be a leaven in society. I want to be an active part of that leaven. I trust you to help me. Amen.

Contemplatio

Lord, make me an apostle!

Thursday of the Fourteenth Week
of Ordinary Time

⋮· · · · · · · · · · · ·⋮

Lectio

Matthew 10:7–15

Meditatio

> *"As you go, make this proclamation:*
> *'The Kingdom of heaven is at hand.'"*

The Gospel of Matthew has used nearly identical phrasing twice before. Matthew first describes John the Baptist's desert ministry: ". . . preaching in the desert of Judea [and] saying, 'Repent, for the kingdom of heaven is at hand!'" (3:1–2). Then Matthew gives us a first glimpse of Jesus' public ministry: "From that time on, Jesus began to preach and say, 'Repent, for the kingdom of heaven is at hand'" (4:17). Now it becomes the initial advice to the Twelve as they are sent out to preach.

"As you go, make this proclamation. . . ." As we go about the day-to-day business of living with others, our words and actions—all the stuff of our daily lives—communicate who we are and what we actually believe in. All those things I promised at Baptism and in my life's commitment sound so simple and straightforward in theory. Do I renounce Satan? Sure. Who wouldn't, right? Do I believe in Jesus Christ? Yes, of course, or I wouldn't be here. Will I pledge my love and fidelity from now until death? With all my heart and strength! I meant it then, and I claim it now—or so I hope. But look at the choices I make when no one else is around; catch my attitude toward the "least" in my estimation; watch me when I'm exasperated with the daily grind . . . and my intentions don't always translate into action. In actual fact, what proclamation am I making?

"The Kingdom of heaven is at hand." Jesus indicates himself as the kingdom of God in person. Jesus is God's authority and God's fidelity to his covenant present in our midst. The kingdom is not some remote country, or a distant event that will happen at the end of the world. It is here now in the person of Jesus Christ.

Oratio

Lord, walk with me in this moment—and in the constant stream of "now" moments of this day—in my every word, gesture, glance, tone, decision. May everything that makes up this day become a ringing proclamation of your kingship in my life. You know the people I will encounter and the decisions I need to make. Open my mind and heart to your grace in this moment, so that I can witness to your graciousness in every moment of today.

Contemplatio

The kingdom of heaven is at hand.

Friday of the Fourteenth Week
of Ordinary Time

⁞· · · · · · · · · · · ·⁝

Lectio

Matthew 10:16–23

Meditatio

> *". . . like sheep in the midst of wolves . . .*
> *shrewd as serpents and simple as doves."*

Any sheep caught in the midst of wolves face grave danger. Jesus warns his apostles of the difficulties they will face in proclaiming the kingdom. But he is our Good Shepherd, so what safety instructions does he give? He uses two additional animal images. First, he says, be shrewd and careful, like a serpent. This may sound odd, since the snake is usually the bad guy in Scripture, on the side of the wolf, not the sheep. For the apostles to become like the serpent would seem to be caving to the pressures of the evil surrounding them. But the second part of the sentence clarifies it—they are to be clever like the serpent, *but* remain innocent of evil, like a dove.

The sheep sent on mission need to be shrewd in order to outsmart the wolves that surround them. Playing with the image a little, we can say they are sent to bring the wolves into the sheepfold. But they must be careful not to take on the ways of the wolves to such a degree that they lose their mission and identity. Their simple innocence prevents that and is part of the witness of their mission. The rest of this passage talks about the persecution that will result, but that they must not allow to sway them from their witness.

Jesus' instructions can be hard to carry out in real life. We may tend to go to extremes and lean more toward the serpent part or the dove part of the instructions. If we're shrewd, we live our Christian life in a way that helps our contemporaries to see the relevance of faith. But if we go too far in learning from the ways of the world around us, we can lose our identity and our mission. However, the answer is not to go too far the other way and become naive doves. In that case we might keep our faith, but nullify its influence and power by a poor witness that alienates our contemporaries.

Oratio

Jesus, you sent me to live my faith in a world that often seems antagonistic to you. Sometimes I do feel like a sheep, with no teeth and claws to protect me—not even legs that run very fast! But you are my Shepherd, so I do not fear. I know you will provide for me whatever I need to do the mission for which you sent me.

Contemplatio

The Lord is my Shepherd.

Saturday of the Fourteenth Week of Ordinary Time

⦂············⦂

Lectio

Matthew 10:24–43

Meditatio

". . . do not be afraid; you are worth more than many sparrows."

Jesus has just commissioned his apostles, giving them detailed instructions for their preaching. He has also given them some dire warnings about the persecutions they will face as they proclaim the kingdom. They are to be afraid only of the one "who can destroy both body and soul in Gehenna."

Today's Gospel also gives us some of Jesus' words of encouragement to the small band of apostles. They are to speak in the light and proclaim from the housetops. They will need to recall the Father's care for the sparrows, knowing that they are worth more than many sparrows. They are to believe firmly that, in losing their lives for Jesus' sake, they will find them. People who assist them will receive their reward, even if they only give them a cup of cold water.

When I consider Jesus' clear instructions, I wonder what a public relations person would think of it all. If I were in that group of disciples, would I have stayed the course with all those warnings and admonitions? Then Jesus' words shine in the depths of my soul: "You are worth more than many sparrows." I begin to see what an impression Jesus left in the hearts of his first followers. The love and loyalty he asked of them could never be compared to the fidelity and self-emptying love he had for each one of them.

Jesus had called these men, and they had left all to follow him. I think of the great magnetism Jesus must have radiated from his heart, so full of love for all people. The strength and loyalty of this love far outshone the difficulties Jesus predicted would come their way. They were going to spread the Good News about a Person. They would spread this message by the contagion of their enthusiasm and the zeal of their preaching. Their lives would never again be the same—nor would ours!

Oratio

Jesus, your words were carved on the hearts of your disciples, and the message they spread has been stamped on my life, too. I ask for their same loyal love and steadfast courage as I go about the works of your kingdom in my own small corner of your world.

Contemplatio

"For it will not be you who speak but the Spirit of your Father speaking through you" (Mt 10:20).

Fifteenth Sunday of Ordinary Time — Year A

∴ · · · · · · · · · · · · ∴

Lectio

Matthew 13:1–23

Meditatio

"A sower went out to sow."

Have you ever planted a garden? I have . . . with many and varied results! Gardening has given me a great respect for the fragility of the seed and the importance of the weather, the amount of moisture, and sunlight. Then there is the timing! It takes a lot of patience and care to do anything in the garden, but gardening has wonderful rewards.

I wonder how God, the Divine Gardener, looks at me, his garden? Surely when God looks at me, he surveys the land with an expert eye. I am in good, capable hands. In fact, I can entrust myself completely to these hands. God knows me through and through. The Divine Gardener knows how much light I need, how much water and sun. My good God is completely solicitous that I should grow in a way that will be fully according to my nature. He is patient enough to walk with me through all the seasons of my life, even when some are more fallow than others. Through it all, God makes me bear divine fruits through his Son, Jesus Christ

God has given me so much and has been so considerate of me. Even when bad things happen, God walks with me and can bring good out of the situation. God never wills evil, but we live in an imperfect world where we choose the wrong way at times. We can be enticed by evil, and we even get sick and die. Yet evil does not have the last word; it cannot overpower the light. Our God sows the life and light that overcome all obstacles. He gives each one of us what we need.

In the presence of the Sower, I pause and recall the blessings that the Lord has put in my life. In a grateful response to the Divine Gardener, I will nurture another person today. I will be light. The Lord will surely send me someone who needs my help.

Oratio

Lord Jesus, you trusted so fully in your Father's love. You placed yourself entirely into his hands. Help me trust completely that he is always with me, watering the land that is my small garden and preparing the way for a fruitful harvest. I am able to give to others because of the fruit of God's love in my life. No matter what happens, I know that God is with me and will teach me through all that happens. I ask for light and wisdom to see with the eyes of faith today and always.

Contemplatio

"Blessed are your eyes, because they see, and your ears, because they hear."

Fifteenth Sunday of Ordinary Time — Year B

∴ · · · · · · · · · · · ∴

Lectio

Mark 6:7–13

Meditatio

> *". . . to send them out two by two . . ."*

Why two by two? If Jesus had sent the Twelve out individually, they could have gone to more places and encountered more people.

Going out two by two allows for mutual support and the opportunity not only to preach the Good News, but also to witness to it by the way they treat each other. They can support each other in the sense that they can decide together what to do in unforeseen circumstances. They can remind each other of Jesus' instructions and care for each other in case of injury or sickness. Being together gives them greater protection from danger during travel.

Forming a small community of two also gives the apostles an opportunity to witness to the mutual love that Jesus expects of them. We can profit from their example in our lives, too. It might seem more expedient to do something alone, but collaboration, joint efforts, and group projects often offer invaluable benefits.

Yes, a mother can make cookies faster by herself than when her four-year-old is "helping" her. But what would be lost? The child enjoys benefits ranging from development of motor skills and a love of cooking, to a confidence in being loved and valued. The mother receives helpful practice in patience and the happiness of seeing her child find joy. Both of them experience the bond of growing love.

Yes, a pastor of a parish can more quickly plan an event by deciding everything himself than by discussing it with a team of parishioners. But if he involves others, he gains an opportunity for greater participation, with people doing what they do best. He gains greater insight, inspiration, and richness, and a growth in the communion and mutual appreciation in the parish.

Oratio

Jesus, sometimes I feel that it would be easier to fly solo. Working with others requires long discussions, practicing patience, trying to see things from others' point of view, and giving up my own opinions. All these things require time and effort, but they lead to growth in holiness and a richer outcome. Help me to value others more and be open to the ways your Spirit works through the community of people with whom I live.

Contemplatio

Where two or three are gathered in the name of Jesus, he is there.

Fifteenth Sunday of Ordinary Time — Year C

❖ · · · · · · · · · · · · ❖

Lectio

Luke 10:25–37

Meditatio

". . . a Samaritan . . ."

As followers of Christ we are called to a high standard of love. I was especially impressed by something that happened at the Superdome in New Orleans in the aftermath of Hurricane Katrina. As help was arriving to rescue people, many pushed forward—even violently—to be taken first. A small group of Vietnamese Catholics quietly remained in their places, praying the rosary, asking that the *others* be taken first. Another moving example occurred in October 2006, when the Amish community in Pennsylvania publicly forgave a gunman who had brutally shot and killed five Amish schoolgirls.

When I witness families, communities, and parish committees who have a communication style marked by passive aggression or angry bitterness, I wonder where our high standard of love has gone. How are we different from those who have no faith? We have no gun (usually) so the violence isn't reported in the papers, but it is still hateful violence. Can we still rise to the challenge that Jesus gives us with the parable of the Good Samaritan?

When we hear "Good Samaritan," our hearts are warmed by the gentle kindness of the man who went out of his way to help someone who was down and out. When Jesus' listeners heard "Samaritan," they felt at least intense disgust if not outright hatred. Strong animosity existed between the Jews and the Samaritans. They didn't live together, eat together, pray together, or even communicate. A centuries-long standoff kept the two groups apart. Jesus is saying that the one you hate, the one you think is no good, may be the one who will someday save you. In a way, Jesus is describing himself as the Good Samaritan for the human race. Jesus is also showing us how to behave when we are the labeled outsider, and he is humbling those who label others as good or bad. Finally, Jesus is calling us as his followers to communion, mutual forgiveness, and personal service.

Oratio

Jesus, what you say is hard. I'm not sure I can do this. How can I create communion in the difficult situations in which I live? I hear your answer: "You can't create communion. Only I can. All I ask you to do is to forgive, to serve the other people in your life, even your 'enemies,' and to love everyone."

Contemplatio

All that you ask of me, Lord, I cannot do on my own. I depend on you to accomplish it in me.

Monday of the Fifteenth Week of Ordinary Time

∴ · · · · · · · · · · · · ∴

Lectio

Matthew 10:34–11:1

Meditatio

> *"I have come to bring not peace but the sword."*

The "sword," commentators say, isn't to be taken literally. It's an image for division. However, when Matthew's Gospel was written, Christians were being denounced to the pagan authorities as traitors against the "divine" emperor. Some of them were even betrayed by family members, and the result was indeed death.

In our own twenty-first century, North American culture, violent persecution of our religion is rare. Individuals in general are more tolerant, and many families tend to accept their member's shifts in religious allegiance with little comment.

But as we know, persecution is taking other forms. In society at large, clashes over religious beliefs are becoming more frequent. Manger scenes are less "acceptable" in public places. A teacher might recommend counseling for a child who has chosen to depict the crucified Jesus in art class. A prayer service outside an abortion clinic may be denounced as harassment.

When a moral issue is brought up in the home or workplace, sometimes we would rather not speak out. We hope that our silence will get the message across. Perhaps it will, but not always. Sometimes we have to speak if we're going to be true to our Catholic beliefs.

That's one way the cross comes into our lives today. Our cross will sometimes consist of witnessing to what we believe.

It's tricky—finding a way to present the truth in charity. Usually we ought to presume right intention and goodwill on the part of whoever holds a viewpoint that is counter to Church teaching. If we present the Christian message with kindness, we may eventually draw that person to a different viewpoint and to the Lord himself.

Oratio

Lord Jesus, I ask the strength to profess your teachings as explained by the Church. I recognize this as a cross that will be hard to bear at times. Whenever your Spirit inspires me to speak out, help me to present the truth in charity. Never let me forget that the other party is probably sincere and certainly deserves my respect as a fellow human being, made in your image. Enlighten me as to what to say and do. Amen.

Contemplatio

I want to be your witness, Lord.

Tuesday of the Fifteenth Week
of Ordinary Time

⸭············⸭

Lectio

Matthew 11:20–24

Meditatio

> *"Jesus began to reproach the towns*
> *where most of his mighty deeds had been done. . . ."*

At the time of Jesus, comparing Chorazin, Bethsaida, and Capernaum to Tyre, Sidon, and Sodom would be something like comparing a wholesome Midwestern town to a stereotypical sin city. Capernaum was a fishing village. Bethsaida was the home of the apostles Peter, Andrew, and Philip, according to the Gospel of John. Along with Chorazin, these Galilean towns were full of simple, hard-working people.

It's not recorded that the people of these towns had any shocking collective sins. From what did they need to repent? We may have similar thoughts about ourselves: "I'm living a pretty good life. I don't have any major sins to repent of." So we continue as we are. This is exactly what Jesus is referring to. These towns witnessed many healings and heard his teaching many times. Jesus had done mighty deeds there, such as the dramatic cure of the paralyzed man. How could the townsfolk simply have gone on with their lives as usual? They seemed unimpressed. Or perhaps they had been amazed when they saw Jesus work a cure, but then they went back to daily life as if nothing had happened.

To encounter Jesus and witness his power invites us to change our lives. The kingdom of God is already in our midst. How can we go on with business as usual? Jesus did not come down to earth to entertain the people of Galilee with a show. His mighty deeds were not done to impress them or inspire them. His presence is a sign that something new, something life-changing is happening. Jesus' reproach seems harsh, but he knows the opportunity these towns have been given.

Oratio

Jesus, I don't want to miss the opportunities or invitations you put on my path. You aren't here teaching and working miracles in the way you did in Galilee, but I know you are here working in my life. And you are certainly working in your Church. I think you might be calling me to be part of something in particular, but I haven't gotten involved. I have so much to do already. Did the fishermen of Capernaum feel that way? I don't want you to pass me by. Give me the courage to let you come into my life and stir it up.

Contemplatio

I will look to see where I am being called to make changes in my life.

Wednesday of the Fifteenth Week of Ordinary Time

∴⋯⋯⋯∴

Lectio

Matthew 11: 25–27

Meditatio

> *". . . you have revealed [these things] to the childlike."*

Today's Gospel passage is consoling. It speaks to those of us who may feel that living the spiritual life is beyond our ability. With a myriad of Scripture commentaries available and an even greater array of books and Web articles on prayer, the path to union with God can seem downright intimidating and overwhelming.

But Jesus is telling us that exactly the opposite is true. He's giving us the *Good News* that the way to God is actually uncomplicated. It's not restricted to the educated and elite. It's for everyone. It's for you and me. The only prerequisite for the journey is a spirit of childlike simplicity.

Jesus tells us that the Father has handed everything over to him. Jesus is the one who chooses those to whom he wishes to reveal his Father. And he's chosen to make this magnificent revelation to us! Isn't it a relief to know that we don't need a master's degree in theology or Scripture to really get to know and love Jesus, his Father, and their Spirit? All we need is an open and trusting heart—one that longs for divine light and love.

The Father has been gracious enough to reveal his Son to us, sending him to live among us, and providing us with the Gospels, the Church, and the lived examples and teachings of the saints. Jesus, for his part, has revealed his Father to each of us through his every action and word. Let's praise them both today for the gift of divine revelation. Let's rejoice in the humility and simplicity of spirit that opens us up to God.

Oratio

Jesus, how good and comforting it is to know that you never expect more of me than I have to give. You ask me to come before you and your Father as a child—expectant and full of trust. My neediness and helplessness only serve to attract you to me. Help me to remain childlike in spirit. Show me that the way of simplicity and confidence is also the way to divine knowledge and grace.

Contemplatio

Lord, let me know you more and more!

Thursday of the Fifteenth Week of Ordinary Time

Lectio

Matthew 11:28–30

Meditatio

"For my yoke is easy, and my burden light."

Probably few people reading this book have ever plowed a field with a yoke of oxen, churning the soil to prepare it for planting. But everyone has sat in a classroom, writing in notebooks, taking tests, or watching the hands of the clock sweep off the minutes until the bell would ring. In fact, the classroom image is closer to what Jesus is talking about in today's Gospel passage. Consider this other Scripture text, ". . . gain, at no cost, wisdom for yourselves. Submit your neck to her yoke, that your mind may accept her teaching. For she is close to those who seek her, and the one who is in earnest finds her" (Sir 51:25–26). This text aligns acquiring wisdom with being under a yoke. That image is in the background of Jesus' saying that his burden is light.

Jesus is inviting us to go to his school, the school of wisdom. Today's Gospel needs to be read together with yesterday's, in which Jesus tells us about knowing his Father. Only Jesus reveals the Father to us. That is where wisdom lies. In the school of Jesus, we can learn about what really matters in life. In today's society, education offers people a boost up the ladder of success. That is surely important to pursue in the business of making a living. But what about making a life?

Jesus offers all of us the knowledge that we need to succeed in making a life. In his school, we can all have scholarships and we can all be honor students. He imparts knowledge freely to anyone who wants it. He teaches us about love. He'll ask us to ponder questions like this: at the end of life, how will we see the times we made selfish choices, and the times that we sacrificed ourselves for someone else? On the balance scales of life, love outweighs everything else. Jesus the Teacher will help us tip the scales in the right direction.

Oratio

Jesus, you are the Teacher of truth, Wisdom incarnate. Teach me to value what really matters in life. Don't let me get so caught up in pursuing other things that I forget that love is what counts most. Help me to build up my family relationships and pay attention to the needs of the people around me.

Contemplatio

"Take my yoke upon you and learn from me."

Friday of the Fifteenth Week
of Ordinary Time

⁝············⁝

Lectio

Matthew 12:1–8

Meditatio

> *". . . something greater than the temple is here."*

The Pharisees are disputing with Jesus about his apparent disregard for Sabbath discipline. He allowed his disciples to pick and eat heads of grain, although this activity is prohibited on the Sabbath. Jesus' reply to them seems a bit of one-upmanship. "What about David?" he asks. "What would you have done about the occasion when David led his followers into the house of God and ate the bread that had been offered to God? This was unlawful, too. And the priests serving in the temple on the Sabbath are permitted to break the law of Sabbath rest. In their case the Law says they are innocent."

Jesus then tells them that something greater than the temple is here. What is Jesus referring to as greater than the temple? Is it one of the exceptions he proposed, or is it himself? Perhaps he is playing one on the other, since he is God's exception to the interpretation of the Law. Or is he referring to the virtue of love—the human activity that mirrors the divine most perfectly? "If you knew what this meant, that *I desire mercy, not sacrifice*, you would not have condemned these innocent men." In all of this, he declares himself to be the Son of Man, a significant title of the Messiah. He is the Lord of the Sabbath and therefore, master of its regulations, the maker of exceptions—not frivolous exceptions made for their own sake, but exceptions made in view of the greatest law. Even the Law is subservient to the Lord. It is the servant of God's glory and of the love we owe one another for God's sake.

This utterance of the Lord is a preview of Matthew 22:34–40, in which Jesus declares that the whole Law is summed up by the law of love, and that this Great Commandment, when regarding others, equals mercy. To think kindly of, to support, to bear with, to overlook the transgressions of another is harder and a more pleasing gift to give God than sacrifices.

Oratio

Preserve me, Lord, from being an inconsistent disciple. Let me absorb your word and live it out sincerely. You pointed to the two loves as equally important, because the second allows us to show our love for you. Keep me focused on living out my love for you and my neighbors. Don't let me get lost in quibbling over who is doing what, but rather let me consider what will please you. Amen.

Contemplatio

It is mercy I desire and not sacrifice.

Saturday of the Fifteenth Week
of Ordinary Time

∴ · · · · · · · · · · · ∴

Lectio

Matthew 12:14–21

Meditatio

"He will not contend or cry out . . ."

Jesus has just healed a man with a shriveled hand. In the process he has a dispute with the Pharisees. At the beginning of today's Gospel passage, these men who seriously lived according to the laws of their religion "went out" and began to plot the death of Jesus, who to them is obviously not concerned with keeping the Law.

What amazement! Jesus doesn't descend into arguing with them. He doesn't withdraw to protect himself or to hide. He doesn't try to reframe his message so it will be more palatable to those plotting his death. Instead he withdraws and quietly carries on with healing, not just one person as in the last healing story, but healing "them all."

Have you lived in a situation in which you or your plans and beliefs were being attacked? It takes enormous strength of character not to descend into arguing, rationalizing, pleading, capitulating, or just plain being nasty tempered. We might express our ugly or angry feelings to safe persons outside the situation. Nevertheless, a cycle of antipathy and ill will can be started that is difficult to break. And in the end nothing good is accomplished. Sometimes groups have to be dissolved, friendships ruined, marriages broken apart.

Jesus shows us another way. He quietly goes forward doing what his Father has sent him to do. "He will not contend or cry out, nor will anyone hear his voice in the streets." I remember once being angry at a group of people who were angry with me. A sister I was working with just laughed and said that was the way it was with this group. Her pleasant attitude shocked me as I realized that it was possible to react differently in the situation. She taught me by her attitude how to be like Jesus, how not to get wrapped up in the problem so much that I could no longer see what had to be done. It was a lesson that freed me from a lot of negative energy.

Oratio

Jesus, I too have a mission. My life has meaning. I am here for others. Make me capable of gently pursuing the will of God for me. Don't let me get caught in a negative cycle, but show me a way out into the wide expanse of goodness and trust.

Contemplatio

I adore you, Jesus, gentle Healer and good Master.

Sixteenth Sunday of Ordinary Time —
Year A

⠲⠄⠄⠄⠄⠄⠄⠄⠄⠄⠄⠄⠄⠄⠂

Lectio

Matthew 13:24–43

Meditatio

"The kingdom of heaven may be likened to . . ."

What is the kingdom of God? Is it a place, a thing, a way of living? Throughout the Gospels, Jesus uses parables to describe what the kingdom of heaven is like. In this passage he offers us several images. The kingdom is like "a man who sowed good seed in his field . . . a mustard seed that a person took and sowed in a field . . . yeast that a woman took and mixed with three measures of wheat flour."

What do these images have in common? Each of them concerns a person who is doing something—sowing seeds in a field, mixing yeast into flour. The person initiates the action. The person takes something very small—a seed, a piece of yeast—and mixes it into a larger reality—a field, several measures of flour.

What could Jesus be saying to us about the kingdom of heaven? Could he be describing God and his action in my life and in the world? Perhaps he is describing the reality of God who is our Father and who in silent, subtle, and yet powerful ways works to penetrate our individual human lives and human history. He thus transforms us from within and allows his reign, his kingdom, to gradually come about in us and in the world.

What does that mean for my life today? The Father wants to be involved in my life. He wants to share his very life of love and grace with me. He wants to penetrate all parts of my human existence with himself. But he chooses to do so with small, daily steps. At first they may be imperceptible, but ultimately they will have deep and lasting effects. Although we may be tempted at times to doubt it, God is involved in our lives, in the life of our world, and he has one goal: to transform you and me and all of humanity!

Oratio

Jesus, in a world where so many people think that if God exists he is surely uninterested and uninvolved in our lives, you reveal to us the Father who is deeply at work through all the details of our daily life. Thank you for teaching us and showing us through your life that the Father desires only to draw us into himself. This is his kingdom—that faithful, loving relationship with him, of which we are all invited to be a part. Help me to be attentive to the ways the Father is bringing about his kingdom in my life today. Help me to "second" his action through a humble, docile, and trusting spirit.

Contemplatio

Master, may your kingdom come!

Sixteenth Sunday of Ordinary Time —
Year B

⁚ · · · · · · · · · · · ⁚

Lectio

Mark 6:30–34

Meditatio

> "*. . . they had no opportunity even to eat.*
> *So they went off in the boat by themselves . . . .*"

In today's Gospel, Jesus invites the apostles to find a quiet place for some well-deserved relaxation. But the crowds rush there, and when Jesus arrives, he sees the urgent needs of the people waiting for him, and he ministers to them. So it seems that Jesus lets them override the less important needs of the disciples for rest and nourishment. But is that really what is occurring?

Let's imagine what happens after Jesus and his disciples leave in the boat. On the shore, as soon as the boat pulls away, word begins to spread that Jesus has left and is on his way to a certain place. People from all the towns around there get to know about it. Crowds of people begin walking to the location. In the boat, the disciples have probably brought something to eat, since they haven't had a chance to eat until now. They must be enjoying a leisurely voyage with Jesus, eating and relaxing with him as the boat rides the gentle swells of the Sea of Galilee. Because the crowds of people arrive beforehand, Jesus and the apostles are probably not sailing or rowing the boat at any great pace.

When Jesus disembarks, a vast crowd is waiting. ". . . his heart was moved with pity for them, for they were like sheep without a shepherd; and he began to teach them many things."

So it seems that the lesson is not that Jesus sacrifices his own fundamental needs and those of his disciples to minister to the people. He does, in fact, do that many times, but perhaps what we learn here is that Jesus can satisfy every need, no matter how pressing or prosaic. Then, having had our needs fulfilled by Jesus, we must be willing to turn around and give to others, as we have received.

Oratio

Jesus, I know that it's important for me to take care of myself physically, emotionally, and spiritually. I also know that sometimes I am called on to sacrifice my own needs for the good of others. It's not always easy to know which needs come first. Sometimes I fail in both directions. Help me learn when to take the time to relax with you in the boat, and when to be generous and unselfish in giving of my time and resources to help others who need me.

Contemplatio

Jesus, you are my fulfillment.

Sixteenth Sunday of Ordinary Time— Year C

⋮ . . . . ⋮

Lectio

Luke 10:38–42

Meditatio

". . . you are anxious and worried about many things."

Let's imagine the scene: in one room Jesus is speaking to his disciples. One of his dearest friends, Mary, the sister of Martha, sits at his feet listening attentively. Martha, who had welcomed Jesus to her home, is working in the next room that serves as a kitchen, busily preparing the meal. As she works, she keeps looking over at the circle of disciples, and becomes more and more agitated. She's alone doing *all* the serving. Martha goes from one pot to another, fussing and growing more angry and resentful. Mary is just sitting there, unconcerned about all the work that needs to be done. Martha's resentment fuels her frantic work. Finally, she bursts into the room to speak her mind to Jesus and ask him to do something. Instead of telling Mary to get up and help, Jesus points out to Martha that she is "anxious and worried about many things." He knows she loves him too, but in her service for him she is focusing on the burden she is carrying, rather than on what is really important. Mary has chosen to listen with love and humility to the word of Jesus. Martha's frenetic activity has, for the moment, sapped her of her love and her peace of mind and heart.

We, too, are often plagued by worry and anxiety in our family setting, workplace, and even our prayer life. How can we escape from our worries and endless activity and find peace of mind and heart? Jesus invites us to pause and make our priorities clear, to seek first his will for us, and to spend some time with him. The word of God gently yet powerfully penetrates our minds and hearts, and keeps us focused on our relationship with God. We all do so many things, but our motives can make us feel anxious—or they can help us feel at peace with ourselves and God. It all depends on where we have set our priorities. Martha was serving the Lord, but other "things" distracted her from the "better part" that could also be hers.

Oratio

Lord, I want to take today as an opportunity to reassess my priorities. I want to take time today for spiritual and physical renewal. Sunday is a day for the "better part," but I so often spend it like any other day. I want my relationship with you to grow and deepen. May it be a balm or spiritual ointment to lessen my anxieties and build up my trust in your care for me. Bless and complete what I have begun. Amen.

Contemplatio

Lord, your kingdom come, your will be done.

Monday of the Sixteenth Week
of Ordinary Time

∴ · · · · · · · · · · · · ∴

Lectio

Matthew 12:38–42

Meditatio

> *". . . and there is something greater . . . here."*

As we follow Jesus' ministry in Matthew's Gospel, it may seem strange to us that the scribes and Pharisees are asking for a sign. In chapter 12 alone, Jesus has healed the man with the withered hand and cured a demoniac. He has been working many miracles. So why are they asking again for a sign?

Based on the Pharisees' assertion in Matthew 12:24 that Jesus is casting out demons through allegiance with the prince of demons, it seems likely that the Pharisees are asking Jesus to offer proof, or a sign, that he is really from God. In substance, they are saying, "Where does your power really come from? And if from God, then prove it." Imagine the consternation of Jesus, who so deeply longs to reach each person's heart. Here he is, preaching a Gospel of love and repentance, healing the sick, and casting out demons. If the reality of what he is doing doesn't offer his audience proof that the power of God is in their midst, then what will?

Yet aren't our own hearts at times just as impregnable to God's presence around us as those of the Pharisees? I know I can be blind to a God who defies my expectations, revealing himself in hidden, sometimes paradoxical ways. Yet God did not cease to dwell with us when Jesus died on the cross. That was only the beginning. The resurrected Lord continues to dwell with us and within us today. Do we believe this?

"There is something greater . . . *here*." Right here, today, we have access to something greater than the preaching of the prophets or the wisdom of the legendary King Solomon. There *is* something greater here, and that something is a *Someone*—it is the Christ, our Lord and our God!

Oratio

Jesus, help me to grow ever more aware of your presence within and around me. Help me to see the ways that the power of God continues to work today, weaving a thread of the divine through every situation and person I encounter. You are rarely what I expect, yet you are more than I can imagine. Allow me to remain open to the mystery of who you are, and to the manifold and mysterious ways you choose to reveal yourself—especially those ways that may defy my expectations and hopes.

Contemplatio

"My Lord and my God!"

Tuesday of the Sixteenth Week
of Ordinary Time

⠒⠄⠄⠄⠄⠄⠄⠄⠄⠄⠄⠄⠒

Lectio

Matthew 12:46–50

Meditatio

> ". . . whoever does the will of my heavenly Father . . ."

Have you ever found yourself admiring other persons for their strength, patience, noble character, or goodness of heart? "Wow, they are truly blessed," we might think. "They certainly have it all together." Admiration is appropriate when we witness the best in others, but looked at from another perspective, admiration lets us off the hook. The others are admirable for what they have chosen to do or be. Admiration often implies that others are far above us, doing something we could never aspire to. We might think we live in another realm, one that is mediocre and humdrum. So we can't expect ourselves to be as great as the ones we admire.

Like the woman in today's Gospel who admired the mother of Jesus, we too might be tempted to only worship, adore, and admire the Son of this mother. While there is nothing wrong with that, Jesus quickly calls us to something deeper:

I, Jesus says, am the *yes* of God. Spoken by the Father as the Word, I am one with the Father in obedience and complete, responsive love. Mary is the highest model in the human race of *yes*. Without hesitation, consideration, calculation of what it would cost or how she would perform, she simply surrendered her entire life, her body, her future to the Father, desiring that the will of God be completely fulfilled in her. You are most truly yourself when you become yes. And you can make this choice for yes.

Jesus says, don't admire those who had physical contact with me during my life on earth. That physical proximity does not give them an edge over you. You have the same possibility as they did to be *yes*. Open your heart, your life, your mind, your desires, your words, your actions to the Father, becoming an empty canvas upon which he draws. Become the "handmaiden of the Lord." Allow the story of salvation to be accomplished in you and through you. Without hesitation, say yes to all that God wills in your life.

Oratio

Jesus, yes of the Father, it is not as easy as it sounds to say yes. I'm afraid of the unknown. I want to control my life. I like adventures but not those that put my career or dreams at risk. Still, that is what makes this yes so powerful. The writings of the saints are full of this invitation to complete surrender to your Father . . . and mine. From this moment on, my Lord, I say yes.

Contemplatio

From this moment on, my Lord, I say yes.

Wednesday of the Sixteenth Week
of Ordinary Time

⋮· · · · · · · · · · · ·⋮

Lectio

Matthew 13:1–9

Meditatio

"And [Jesus] spoke to them at length in parables . . ."

I picture the day in my mind's eye: the blue sky, the rocky shore, the waves bobbing the boat that holds Jesus, the crowd of people hanging on his words. Jesus speaks, and his words float out over the crowd like a soft breeze of the Spirit.

What refreshment the teaching of Jesus gives these people, whose lives are burdened with cares, sickness, financial worries, even the tragedies that can stop a person cold with heartbreak . . . . They feel as if Jesus is addressing them individually, and really, he *is*. Jesus' Good News is miraculous in many ways. But the way it has penetrated to the hearts of people all over the world through the ages is a miracle that goes on continually.

I think of the way my life was changed as I heard or read Jesus' Sermon on the Mount or his seven last words from the cross. For a moment, I feel a sense of connection with Jesus' audience on that shore in Palestine.

Jesus preferred parables when teaching the people, who could easily learn to use the book of nature as a springboard to the deep realities that he presented. I can do this, too. The Holy Spirit's gift of understanding helps me to go in faith from created realities to their Creator.

Then the "soil" of my soul will be fertile ground for the seed of the Good News that the Lord sows in my life.

Oratio

Jesus, enlighten me with the wisdom of your Gospel, you who alone have the words of everlasting life. Help me to be good soil for the seed of your teaching. Nourish that seed with your grace, so that it will grow and flourish as I resolve to live for your kingdom.

Contemplatio

"Whoever has ears ought to hear."

Thursday of the Sixteenth Week
of Ordinary Time

∴ · · · · · · · · · · · ∴

Lectio

Matthew 13:10–17

Meditatio

> *"They . . . hear but do not listen or understand. . . .*
> *But blessed are . . . your ears."*

The disciples have asked Jesus why he often speaks in parables. His answer seems to suggest that he doesn't want the crowd to grasp the meaning of his words and be saved. But Scripture is a unity; its parts are harmonious. Elsewhere Scripture says: "God . . . wills everyone to be saved" (1 Tim 2:3–4). So, whatever Jesus' meaning was, his parables must have been meant for the good of the people of his time and place. Perhaps he spoke in parables so that some people could mull over his words before making a decision, and others could ignore the message until they were ready to respond to it later on.

In any case, how does this passage relate to us?

Recently I was struck by the contrast between the two groups of hearers, those who ponder the words and those who set aside the message for later. And I was startled by this insight: Which group do I belong to?

It could be that in searching for the original meaning of Jesus' words, I'm not hearing what he's saying to me here and now. Perhaps I'm only trying to discover the literal meaning grasped by the original hearers or the evangelist. Pope Benedict and others point out that even though it's important to search for the original, literal meaning, Scripture also has other dimensions.

God's word is *alive today*. Whether I attend Mass in person, watch it on TV, or simply read Scripture at home, God wants to speak to me personally through his word.

Commentaries are certainly helpful, as are books of prayerful reflections on Scripture. They can stimulate my own pondering—and that's what they're meant to do. They can help me prepare to receive the Lord's here-and-now word for me at this time and in this place. But I have to be *open to receive* that word, giving the Holy Spirit an opportunity to communicate the message he wants me to hear.

May my ears be "blessed."

Oratio

Jesus, Word of the Father, help me to open myself to your message. May I not close my ears too soon, thinking I've already heard what you want to tell me through a particular passage. Teach me to give the Spirit time for his inspirations to stir my heart.

Contemplatio

Holy Spirit, teach me how to really listen.

Friday of the Sixteenth Week of Ordinary Time

∴∙∙∙∙∙∙∙∙∙∙∙∴

Lectio

Matthew 13:18–23

Meditatio

". . . the seed sown . . ."

In today's reading Jesus explains the parable of the sower, found in all three Synoptic Gospels. Speaking to people who till the soil, Jesus uses images familiar to his hearers. A sower goes out to plant seeds and some of them yield a good crop, but others do not. It all depends on the type of soil where the seeds fall.

Biblical scholars explain that in this parable the sower represents Christ, and the seed is the word of God, or the preaching of the kingdom. The evil one is Satan. The soil symbolizes the heart of each person with its receptivity to the word. Some hearts will accept it, while others will suffocate or even reject the word.

Which kind of *soil* am I?

Some people do not respond to the preaching of the word. They make no effort to understand and practice what they hear. The seed is plucked away and does not yield any fruit. *Am I this shallow soil?*

Other individuals are easily won over when they hear the word. But when problems come, or when they are persecuted because of their beliefs, they close their hearts and the seed dies. *Am I this hardened, rocky soil?*

Still others let themselves become so entwined with wealth, worldly distractions, and the desire to make a name for themselves, that the seed is suffocated. *Am I this matted, entangled field?*

But others hear the word and respond to it with all their hearts. They joyfully accept the word and the challenges of God's kingdom. The seed produces an abundant harvest in their lives. *Am I this moist, rich, productive soil?*

Oratio

Lord Jesus, may the ground of my life be well tilled and prepared to receive your word. I want to welcome you into a heart that is open, receptive, loving. In this way, my life will bear a plentiful, bounteous harvest, with your help, and for your glory.

Contemplatio

I welcome your word in my heart.

Saturday of the Sixteenth Week of Ordinary Time

∴···········∴

Lectio

Matthew 13:24–30

Meditatio

"Let them grow together until harvest . . ."

In this parable we see our world's reality. All around us are signs of the good seed that has been sown. So many kind and generous people have responded well to God's invitations and dedicated themselves to helping others. Perhaps we can recognize some of these people in our own families or faith communities and among our friends and coworkers.

Similarly we may notice others who seem to lack these motivations or goodness, whose actions and choices cause grief and do harm. Some slip into bad habits and evil ways for a time but turn again to the path of virtue. Others go from bad to worse, spiraling downward into a life of sin and vice.

The more impulsive among us might wish to rebuke, punish, and rid the world of "those evil-doers," but today's parable clearly indicates another approach. Letting the wheat and the weeds grow together for a time is a much gentler and more patient approach. Perhaps the weeds allow the wheat to grow stronger. Likewise, those among the weeds might benefit from the example and prayers of the virtuous.

A profound look into our own hearts might also reveal that while we desire to be the good wheat, we may need to do some pruning right here in our own field. While we live we can always hope that both we and others may correspond to the graces offered by our patient, loving God.

The day of reckoning, however, will come for both the "weeds" and the "wheat." While time is given for repentance and conversion, we will have to answer to God for the way we have lived. We must take seriously the call to reform and return with our whole heart to the Lord while we still have time.

Oratio

Help me, Jesus, to be the "good soil" where the seeds of your word will take root and produce abundant fruit. May I give you glory by accepting your call to grow in virtue and grace. Give me a humble, contrite heart so that I might recognize my sins and turn again to accept your merciful forgiveness.

May I remain strong in my Christian faith even if others around me oppose it. Let my life bear witness to you and become a sign of your saving presence at work in our world. May all who do not know you or live according to your teachings have the grace of repentance and conversion. Lord, give me wisdom to know when charity requires me to speak up on behalf of justice and truth.

Contemplatio

Behold, such is the tender compassion of our God.

Seventeenth Sunday of Ordinary Time
—Year A

⁝ · · · · · · · · · · · ⁝

Lectio

Matthew 13:44–52

Meditatio

"Do you understand all these things?"

This question is important for *us* also to answer. To read or listen to the word of God is to encounter Jesus. He is the one who proclaims the word, and *he* is the one who is proclaimed. At each reading, the word questions us. Jesus asks us just as much as he asked the apostle, "Do you understand all these things?"

Jesus has been talking about the reign of God. Asking if we have understood his words indicates the importance Jesus gives to discernment, being able to notice where we have stumbled upon the reign of God. When we hear these parables we may think of them as once-in-a-lifetime occurrences: they are often used to refer to a religious vocation. However, each of us every day has the possibility of finding the reign of God anew, and we need to make a decision about what we will do with our discovery.

The man who finds a buried treasure realizes the value of his discovery, and sells everything else to make it his own. That is one way we discover the reign of God in daily life. A sudden inspiration, a movie that makes us rethink our values, an example of a virtuous friend can all be like finding a buried treasure. We can keep walking and ignore a painful realization about ourselves or a challenging call to conversion, but this treasure is worth claiming for our own. The merchant searching for fine pearls, on the other hand, has made it his life's work to search among the fine things of life for something authentically valuable. These pearls may look very much alike, but the merchant's trained eye can tell a fake pearl from a real one. Truly valuable pearls are of immeasurable value. We need to seek among the beautiful things in life for what is truly good, beautiful, and true. Appearances can be deceiving, but with discernment and practice we can consistently recognize the pearls that are worth selling all else to obtain.

Oratio

Jesus, I will never find treasure if I don't make it my practice to pursue virtue, holiness, and heroic love of you and others. Help me to be alert to the buried treasure and the fine pearls in my life: inspirations, opportunities, challenges, graces, times of intense prayer, and celebration of the sacraments. I understand that you are calling me to the heights of holiness. Help me. Amen.

Contemplatio

Today I choose the reign of God.

Seventeenth Sunday of Ordinary Time
—Year B

∴ · · · · · · · · · · · ∴

Lectio

John 6:1–15

Meditatio

"Gather the fragments left over, so that nothing will be wasted."

The Apostle Philip has always intrigued me. He's seldom in the limelight, but in John's Gospel he's often *there*. He shows up in chapters 1, 12, and 14, as well as here in chapter 6, where Jesus asks his opinion about how to feed the enormous crowd. I wonder whether Philip was the source for this account of the multiplication of the loaves.

One of the outstanding details in John's account is Jesus' command to gather the fragments of bread, lest anything be wasted. (The Synoptics simply state that the fragments were collected.) It has been pointed out that this refers to the Eucharistic species and the reverence due to it. I think this command can also serve as a reminder not to waste.

In an affluent culture it's easy to be wasteful without even realizing it. We might be careful to recycle containers and conscientious about food, drink, and even clothes, but then there are electricity, water, and even *time*. . . .

Most of us spend much time running errands, commuting and/or waiting (for a bus to arrive, a computer to warm up, traffic lights to change, supper to cook . . .). Part of this time can be spent tuning in to the Lord. As I write this I'm traveling in an interstate bus. A few minutes ago on an elevated stretch of highway we passed through an area where church steeples rose on all sides, signaling the presence of the Eucharist—Jesus in the midst of his people. I'm sure the Lord is pleased when we remember that he's as truly present here among us now as he was on that green hillside where he multiplied the loaves.

Oratio

Lord Jesus, living in the Eucharist throughout the world, I want to remember more often your presence among us and within us. We are never "alone," unless we want to be. It's we, not you, who sometimes break the connection. I ask the Holy Spirit to keep me aware of your presence, especially when I need encouragement, guidance, or strength. But I want to also remember your presence when I don't have particular needs. At times I want to keep the connection open by simply saying, "Thank you, Lord!"

Contemplatio

"Eucharist" means "thanksgiving."

Seventeenth Sunday of Ordinary Time
—Year C

∵∴∵

Lectio

Luke 11:1–13

Meditatio

"When you pray, say: Father . . ."

I once read that all the sound waves of our earth go out into the cosmos. If we could invent a "collector" strong enough, we could conceivably collect and listen to Jesus, in person, praying the Our Father. Be that as it may, I think the apostles were spellbound to witness Jesus' absorption and joy in prayer, and as friends would, asked him to show them how to do this. Jesus gave us a precious jewel that can never be surpassed in beauty and meaning when he gave us this prayer.

As our Redeemer, the Lord Jesus is Healer, and he heals us in the deepest parts of our being, in our relationships. Jesus shares his heavenly Father with us. He shares the relationship that forms the core of the life of the Godhead with us. He wants us to know the Father as *Our* Father, to begin the lifelong quest for this awareness with the words of this prayer. A child can say this prayer, and Jesus wants us to realize that we will always be the children of the heavenly Father. The Father will feed us, forgive us, help us to forgive others, and protect us from trials that would overwhelm us. This relationship is so fundamental that Jesus wants his followers to have the security of his Father's love as the grounds of their being.

How many children, for various sad reasons, have not experienced the protection and care of their fathers or mothers and feel themselves to be painfully alone, sometimes for their entire lives? Even with a healthy upbringing, a person can often feel alone.

We can always turn to our Heavenly Father, who waits for us to ask, seek, and knock. He waits, not with censure, but with attentive, eternal love. He waits, not with goodies, but with eternal life and joy. He waits, not to deny us, but to give the Holy Spirit to those who ask him!

Oratio

Father, when I use the prayer Jesus gave us, I feel somehow that I am slipping my hand into yours, and that I will be safe. Life then becomes easier, because I face it with you. I thank you for sending Jesus to redeem us and let us know our real identities, that we are all your children. I ask your Son and my Savior to help me to grow in likeness to you, so that when I arrive at the shores of eternal life, it will be a true and eternal homecoming.

Contemplatio

". . . how much more will the Father in heaven give the Holy Spirit to those who ask him?"

Monday of the Seventeenth Week of Ordinary Time

∴ · · · · · · · · · · · · ∴

Lectio

Matthew 13:31–35

Meditatio

"The kingdom of heaven is like . . ."

If we were to describe the beauty of a sunset to a blind person, we might try to compare the sunset's beauty to objects and experiences familiar to that person. Still, any explanation of ours would fail to communicate the depth of its beauty, because the person simply wouldn't be able to see the sunset with his or her own eyes.

I wonder if this was Jesus' experience as he tried to explain the kingdom of God to his listeners. Many people were expecting that the Messiah would overthrow the Roman occupation and establish God's kingdom on earth as a powerful kingdom with military and political might. But the images Jesus gives us in this Gospel reveal that to recognize the kingdom of God in our midst, we need to move away from images of domination and power and move toward the hiddenness of the mustard seed and the yeast.

So often, in our time too, we expect to find God in extraordinary events, in the "bolts of lightning." We expect him to act boldly and forcefully in our lives. These expectations can sometimes prevent us from recognizing him when he comes through quiet, seemingly ordinary moments of grace. In the midst of the noise and distractions that vie for our attention, it can be easier to pay attention to extraordinary events and displays of power. We need to find ways of pausing and quieting ourselves so we can welcome the signs surrounding us that point to the kingdom of God.

Oratio

Jesus Master, help me to remember that your ways are not my ways. Help me to recognize when my expectations of how you will act in my life and in the world prevent me from welcoming you. May I learn each day how to open my heart to the daily signs of your kingdom in the midst of my world. I want to be ready to receive the gifts of your love that you send me this day.

Contemplatio

"And the Word became flesh and made his dwelling among us" (Jn 1:14).

Tuesday of the Seventeenth Week
of Ordinary Time

❖ · · · · · · · · · · · ❖

Lectio

Matthew 13:36–43

Meditatio

"Then the righteous will shine like the sun . . ."

During World War II, Hungary had largely avoided Nazi pressure to persecute the Jews until the spring of 1944, when Adolf Eichmann arrived on the scene. During six weeks of terror, from mid-May to the end of June 1944, Eichmann sent almost 450,000 Hungarian Jews to their deaths. Yet a Swedish diplomat named Raoul Wallenberg managed to get many Jews out of Hungary on Swedish passports. His tireless efforts saved around 30,000 people. His reward? When the Soviets rolled into Hungary, they took Wallenberg prisoner and he disappeared into a Soviet gulag. No one knows exactly what befell him. Despite efforts to get him released, he was never freed and he died, deserted and alone, in a Soviet prison or labor camp.

A cynic would say that no good deed goes unpunished. But today's Gospel offers comfort to all the Raoul Wallenbergs of the world, and to all those who were herded into cattle cars and dumped into gas chambers. Evil will not triumph.

Evil will not have the last word. No matter the degree to which justice is perverted in this world, justice will be done in the next. In the parable of the weeds and the wheat, Jesus counsels us to have patience now, for we are still in the time of mercy. While it lasts, God never stops calling his wayward children to repentance. But at some point the judgment will come, and the angels will reap the harvest of the earth. Some wrongs will never be righted on this earth. But they will be righted—not in our time, but in God's. And that should reassure us that though it tarries, the day of justice will not be put off forever. The Lord hears the cry of the poor.

Oratio

Jesus, this Gospel makes me fear the day of reckoning, but at the same time I find it comforting. I don't like to dwell on the face of evil in the world. Yet I cannot deny its existence and I can't make sense of it. You tell us quite plainly that the enemy, the devil, is at work in the world sowing seeds of evil. But the power of your love is stronger than the power of evil. In the end, your love will triumph. Lord, I believe in your love and its power to overcome evil. Increase my faith.

Contemplatio

"Explain to us the parable."

Wednesday of the Seventeenth Week of Ordinary Time

∴ · · · · · · · · · · · · ∴

Lectio

Matthew 13:44–46

Meditatio

". . . out of joy . . ."

These two verses are packed with significance for the disciples of Jesus, bringing us joy and encouragement. In describing the kingdom of heaven for us, Jesus gives us not only an image, but also something we can relate to.

First, this description involves two things that are related to each other: a treasure (or pearls), and a seeker. The seeker finds the treasure and makes that treasure the focal point of his or her desire. He or she wants that treasure more than anything else in the world.

But the seeker cannot yet obtain the treasure, because he or she is not prepared to purchase it. So the seeker goes away in order to sell whatever it takes to be able to purchase the treasure.

This parable is about us. We are the ones who have found a treasure. That treasure is the heart of the kingdom: Jesus. But we are not prepared to purchase the treasure, and Jesus does not expect us to be so prepared. The kingdom of heaven consists of the treasure, *and* the seeker, *and* the process of selling what needs to be sold, *and* returning to take possession of the treasure.

Preparedness, or the ability to live all of the demands of the Gospel, is not a requirement for the kingdom of heaven. The preparedness to obtain the treasure is the consequence of the kingdom of heaven. Knowing that we don't have to be completely prepared can give us joy—the fuel that drives us to continue selling what we need even to the point that it hurts. Our unpreparedness, our ongoing letting go of what prohibits us from completely being in possession of the treasure—that *is* the kingdom of heaven.

Oratio

Jesus, you are the treasure I have found, and the pearl I long to possess. Not only are you the treasure, but also the currency and purchaser of what I need to sell. I know that I'm not ready to possess you. I must sell so many things: fear, unkindness, anxiety, anger, sin. Nourish my longing for you, O Lord, so that it may be stronger than these things I need to sell. With each thing I sell I know you will rejoice with me. That too gives me strength to carry on. Amen.

Contemplatio

Jesus, my treasure lies in you.

Thursday of Seventeenth Week
of Ordinary Time

∴ · · · · · · · · · · · · ∴

Lectio

Matthew 13:47–53

Meditatio

"Do you understand all these things?"

In this chapter of Matthew's Gospel, Jesus explains the kingdom of heaven. He has taken the Twelve aside to offer a more intense explanation, first of the weeds and wheat, then of the mustard seed, the buried treasure, and the fine pearls. Now he speaks to them of the wide net thrown out by the fishermen. The Twelve are to be fishers of men—in fact, most of them are fishermen by profession—and they will have to use a large net, throw it out over the waters and haul in as many fish as possible. When they proclaim the kingdom they will have to reach out to as many people as can hear. An attempt will be made to include everyone in the kingdom, but not all will be chosen. As with the fish, a division is made: they "put what is good into buckets. What is bad they throw away."

Jesus is explaining not just the kingdom of God on earth, but also the Last Judgment, when the good and bad will be separated. The wicked will be taken by angels to the "fiery furnace, where there will be wailing and grinding of teeth," in other words, the sufferings of separation and regret.

Jesus paints a vivid picture for the disciples of the urgency of their mission. They must bring his message to everyone—preach it as far and wide as possible so that many people (ourselves included) will accept the Good News and be ready for the great judgment. "Do you understand all these things?" Yes, they say. Then, he says, you must be "like the head of a household who brings from his storeroom both the new and the old." Distribute to your hearers all knowledge: the wisdom of our tradition and the spirit of the Good News. How often do we thank the Master for sending these fishermen, and those others throughout history, to share the heart of his message with us?

Oratio

Dear Master, thank you for providing fishermen who would pursue the catch down through the ages of your Church. Let us docilely receive your word, humbly submit to what you desire, and intelligently live it out in our lives. And may we, inspired by the head of the household in your story, embrace what is new, and treasure what is old in our tradition. Enrich us, mind and heart, so we, too, will become fishers of the men and women of today.

Contemplatio

My mind and heart await your word.

Friday of the Seventeenth Week
of Ordinary Time

⁘ · · · · · · · · · · · ⁘

Lectio

Matthew 13:54–58

Meditatio

" . . . their lack of faith."

This Gospel scene presents Jesus to us after he has traveled around Galilee gaining fame and popularity by teaching with authority and performing mighty deeds. Jesus might have hoped for a warm, supportive welcome from the people of his hometown, who had known him since his youth. But any hope of comfort or sympathy quickly disappears when he is faced with their suspicious questions and lack of faith.

What is this lack of faith? What exactly are they lacking? What is it that his neighbors cannot believe? Could it be that they are stuck in their own narrow ideas of God? Are they so convinced that they know how God should reveal himself that when God *does reveal himself* in a concrete, visible way in Jesus, they can't recognize him?

Perhaps they haven't lived in a relationship with God. To be "in relationship" with someone means that the parties continually reveal themselves to each other. It would be unreasonable to think I really know anyone through and through. The other person always remains somewhat of a mystery to me, no matter how long we have known each other or how much of ourselves we have shared. How much more true is this of God, who is totally other!

Perhaps Jesus' admonition regarding their lack of faith refers to their lack of a living, growing relationship with God. Perhaps Jesus is inviting them to realize that no one has the last word on how God should be, act, or reveal himself. It is we who must remain open, longing to understand who he is and how he acts in our lives and in the world, ready to assent to what he does show us about himself, because he is God.

Oratio

Jesus, sometimes I think I know you. I also think I know who the Father is and can recognize how he acts in my life. But how often I limit you because of my human and somewhat narrow vision. How often I may be lacking in faith because my relationship with you is based on my self-constructed image of you. Help me, instead, to see the reality of yourself that you are revealing to me day by day. Help me to live today open to what you will teach me about yourself, about the Father, about my relationship with you.

Contemplatio

"I do believe, help my unbelief!" (Mk 9:24).

Saturday of the Seventeenth Week of Ordinary Time

⁘ ⋯⋯⋯⋯⋯ ⁘

Lectio

Matthew 14:1–12

Meditatio

". . . he feared the people . . ."

Whoever is attentive to the daily liturgy will come across this horrible story of the death of John the Baptist three times during the year, including its memorial on August 29. You would think once would be enough. Why does the Church repeat it? Perhaps it is because we need to face it. It's a sad story of a pointless death, and we don't want to think about it too much. But if we look at it honestly, we might see something of Herod in ourselves.

Matthew's account has an interesting difference from Mark's version. Mark says that Herod imprisoned John on account of Herodias, but didn't want to kill him and in fact had a strange attraction to listening to him. Matthew ascribes different motives to Herod. He says that Herod wanted to kill him but feared the popular outcry that might result, because the people regarded John as a prophet. Herod did not want people to regard him as a prophet-killer.

Herod Antipas, son of Herod the Great and tetrarch of Galilee and Perea, seems to be a powerful person. He has the power to imprison John and even to execute him. But who is actually more powerful—John bound and in prison, or Herod who acts first from pressure from Herodias, then out of fear for what people will think, and then to save face in front of his guests? Herod is pitiable. He is like the "reed swayed by the wind" (Mt 11:7) that Jesus contrasts to John. John only moves where the Spirit blows. His power comes from an interior freedom to fearlessly do what he is called to do.

Who are we more like? How interiorly free are we? How often do we make decisions based on our values and what we discern God is asking of us? And how often do we instead look outward—at what people will think, or whom we want to get even with, or how to make a good impression?

Oratio

Jesus, Herod is such a despicable character that I don't even want to think that I might be like him in some way. But sometimes I let popular opinion and currents sway my choices. I want to be more like John the Baptist. I want to have the interior freedom to live as who I am—a child of God. Where can I find the self-confidence and faith to live this way? Where can I find the courage? Implant in me the firm conviction of being loved and called by you.

Contemplatio

In making choices today, I want to be interiorly free.

Trinity Sunday—
Year A

⋮·············⋮

Lectio

John 3:16–18

Meditatio

"God so loved the world. . . ."

My first "catechesis" on the Blessed Trinity consisted of geometric designs in a stained glass window at church. When I started religious education, our text was equally impersonal.

More than a generation later, children's catechesis on the Trinity took on a more human dimension. One primary text introduced the Trinity with these words: "The Father is God, and he loves me. The Son is God, and he loves me. The Holy Spirit is God, and he loves me." When I began catechizing children, I was delighted with this new approach, which proclaimed that the Trinity has an intimate role in our lives.

A simple catechesis based on today's Gospel might quote the First Letter of John: "In this way was the love of God revealed to us: God sent his only Son into the world so that we might have life through him. In this is love: not that we have loved God, but that he loved us and sent his Son as expiation for our sins" (I Jn 4:9–10).

How amazing it is that, despite the waywardness of his free creatures, the Father took pity on us and sent his Son to suffer and die for us, so that our sins could be forgiven and we could become God's children! And how consoling it is that the Holy Spirit gives us chance after chance to continue living in grace and eventually to enter the eternal joy of the Trinity!

In return, God asks love for him and for others. "We love because he first loved us. . . . Whoever loves God must also love his brother" (I Jn 4:19, 21).

Love sums up everything. If we love, we'll try to avoid sin, and when we fall, we'll ask forgiveness. If we love, we'll also be willing to suffer something with and for the Lord. And to love is not really difficult, because it's not always a matter of feelings, but of *wanting* to love. God asks what's possible, not something beyond our reach.

Oratio

Father in heaven, who loved the world so much that you gave your only Son, I stand in awe of the goodness of the Trinity. As Saint Paul says, when all people were sinners, Jesus died for us and he continues to intercede for us. The Holy Spirit bears witness that we are your children, Father, and joint heirs with Jesus.

Father, Son, and Spirit, I thank you for everything you have done for me. I love you and ask the grace to love you always more, and my sisters and brothers as well. Amen.

Contemplatio

Thank you, Father, Son, and Holy Spirit!

Trinity Sunday— Year B

∴ · · · · · · · · · · · ∴

Lectio

Matthew 28:16–20

Meditatio

"Go, therefore . . ."

I have noticed that people usually perceive themselves to be in the world, calling out to God. But these two words, "go, therefore," turn that perception around. It is as though the disciples are within the embrace of the Trinity and are being sent into the world.

For forty days following his resurrection, Jesus has moved in and out of the apostles' lives. He has appeared to them unexpectedly, enjoyed breakfast with them on the beach, and breathed into them his Spirit, giving them the power to forgive sins. Gradually he has weaned them from his daily physical presence to a new relationship with him. They will no longer see him or speak with him as they had during those blessed years before his crucifixion and death. Yet they know he is with them still, though in a different way. He is with them, and they are with him. He is in them and they are in him. They are becoming one with him who is the Way, the Truth, and the Life. Through him they also share in a relationship with the Father. They will soon be filled and anointed with his Spirit. And Jesus now exhorts them to *go* into the world.

What difference would it make in your life if you remembered that you are at home in the Trinity's embrace, looking out onto the world? How would this, for instance, change your family life? Would you feel less entangled or confined or overwhelmed by what happens within relationships in your family? Would you have more options? Would it be possible to consider acting differently? Loving differently? Thinking differently?

Would you pray differently if you knew you were already in the Trinity's embrace? Know that you are already at home, and you are already loved. You have already been given everything you need. You are already held with compassion. The striving, the frustration, the methods of prayers would melt away if you knew deeply whose you are . . . already . . . now.

Oratio

Jesus, help me quiet down. I leave the outside world aside and enter within myself. If I hear sounds I let them drop away. If I have worries I let them melt. When thoughts grab my attention I bring my attention back to the depths of my spirit, where there is complete silence. I listen to the beating of your heart. In you I am hidden in the heart of the Trinity. I am held by the Father, filled with the Spirit, one with you. . . .

Contemplatio

Jesus, I see the world through your eyes.

Trinity Sunday—
Year C

∴∙∙∙∙∙∙∙∙∙∙∙∴

Lectio

John 16:12–15

Meditatio

> *". . . the Spirit . . . will guide you to all truth."*

Today we celebrate Trinity Sunday, the feast of our God, who is one God in three Persons: Father, Son, and Holy Spirit. In the Gospel reading, Jesus reveals that the Holy Spirit will guide us to all truth. He explains that "everything that the Father has is mine," and that the Spirit "will take from what is mine and declare it to you." This truth, then, is divine. What an immense gift! The Spirit will teach us divine truth.

When we love someone, we want to know that person better. We love God and are blessed to be able to know God better and to learn divine truths. These satisfy us in a way that the so-called "truths" that surround us in advertising, news media, some forms of entertainment, or in the gossip that often comes to us do not. These might tickle our curiosity or stir our feelings, but they do not satisfy us in the long run. Our hearts are restless when these are the only truths we listen to. It can be hard to ignore them, however, since we are surrounded by their noise. This is why it is so important that we steep ourselves in divine truth. The Holy Spirit will help us.

Jesus taught us divine truth in his words and in the way he lived. We discover these especially in the Gospels and the other books of the New Testament. The Church, which is the Mystical Body of Jesus, also teaches us divine truth. In our following of Christ, it is essential that we prayerfully ponder these truths. The Holy Spirit enables us to open ourselves to them. Gradually they penetrate our minds and hearts, and we begin to act out of them.

Let us ask the Holy Spirit to teach us and to grant us the gifts of wisdom and understanding so that divine truth will permeate us and flourish within us.

Oratio

Divine Holy Spirit, I adore and love you. Thank you for revealing divine truth to us. I love this truth, but sometimes, the noise of other "truths" blocks out your voice. Help me to choose to listen to you. Teach me and enable me to be attentive to you. Give me the grace I need to open my mind and heart to your words. Grant me your gifts of wisdom and understanding, so as to deepen my understanding of divine truth. Transform my way of thinking so that divine truth becomes the foundation of my attitudes, beliefs, and choices.

Contemplatio

Holy Spirit, teach me divine truth.

Corpus Christi—
Year A

❖···········❖

Lectio

John 6:51–58

Meditatio

> ". . . the bread that I will give is my flesh for the life of the world."

Within the eight verses of today's passage from Saint John, we hear Jesus say in seven different ways that those who eat his flesh and drink his blood will have eternal life. The crowd asks, "How can this man give us his flesh to eat?" They question Jesus because they can't imagine eating his flesh or drinking his blood. They question him because they can't understand how Jesus will give his body and blood as food and drink. They do not know that the offering of his body and blood as our food is necessary to complete the sacrifice of the cross. The Eucharist is an essential part of Jesus' sacrifice on Calvary.

I can ask the same question that the crowd did when they heard Jesus speaking about his body and blood. How can Jesus do this? How can he give me his body and blood for food? Unlike the crowd of Jesus' day, as Christians we know about Jesus' sacrifice on the cross. So my question comes from a deep awareness of God's incredible love for me, that

God gave me his only Son to be my salvation and nourishment.

When I receive the body and blood of Christ, I am meant to give myself for others as Jesus did for me. Can *I* do that? Can *I* possibly give so much? As I partake of the Eucharist by eating the body and blood of Christ, how can I in turn give myself to others? How can I offer myself for the life of the world?

The next time you see athletes perform incredible feats and you exclaim, "How did they do that!" remember Jesus' incredible feat of love. We are all meant to be a part of it because Jesus has given us his body and blood as food for eternal life.

Oratio

Jesus, I praise you for the great gift of the Eucharist. Your entire life was about giving life to others. When I think of the way you poured yourself out in love for me and gave yourself as food, I am amazed, and I desire to be united with you. When I receive your Body and Blood, I pray for the grace to join myself to your sacrifice for the life of the world. Let that offering with you begin now.

Contemplatio

"This is my body, given up for you."

Corpus Christi—
Year B

∶∙∙∙∙∙∙∙∙∙∙∙∙∙∙∙∶

Lectio

Mark 14:12–16, 22–26

Meditatio

"*. . . this is my body . . . this is my blood of the covenant . . .*"

Corpus Christi is the wonderful feast of the Body and Blood of Jesus Christ. At the Last Supper, Jesus gave us the incredible gift of his own self in the Eucharist. We celebrate that on Holy Thursday. But the shadows of Good Friday mingle our joy with sorrow. So the Church gives us another feast to celebrate the gift with a complete joy that basks in the afterglow of Easter.

In this Gospel passage, Mark emphasizes that to drink the cup of Christ's blood is to partake in the new covenant. What does this mean? For the ancient peoples, blood was a powerful symbol of life. To drink Christ's blood means that we share in the very life of God. Jesus poured out his blood on the cross to atone for our sins and to unite us to the Father. ". . . the blood of his Son Jesus cleanses us from all sin" (I Jn 1:7).

Because we are so familiar with these ideas, it can become difficult to grasp what is really going on at Mass. It can become routine. When the Pope comes to visit our country, thousands of people flock to get a glimpse of him and hear his words. I've done that too and it's very exciting. Yet, Jesus himself is made present in the Eucharist at every Mass, and where are the crowds straining to get in? Because Jesus has made himself so easily available, we can take his presence for granted.

Today is a good day to think about what the Eucharist means in our lives. Perhaps we might find time to linger awhile after Mass and pray before Jesus present in the tabernacle. He dwells with us out of love, and only asks for our love in return. A prayer by Saint Thomas Aquinas beautifully highlights the mystery of the Eucharist: "O Sacred Banquet, in which Christ is consumed, the memory of his passion is renewed, the soul is filled with grace, and a pledge of future glory is given to us."

Oratio

Jesus, I adore you present in the Blessed Sacrament, in your Body broken for us and your Blood poured out for us. Thank you for this wonderful gift. Don't let me ever take it for granted. When I receive you in Holy Communion, fill my heart with a greater love for you and for my neighbor, that I might pour myself out in loving service. Amen.

Contemplatio

My Lord and my God!

Corpus Christi—
Year C

∴ · · · · · · · · · · · ∴

Lectio

Luke 9:11b–17

Meditatio

" . . . he said the blessing over them, broke them, and gave them . . . ."

Jesus was born in Bethlehem, which according to some means "house of bread," and his first crib was a feeding trough. Now, three decades later, on a green hillside, he performs the same actions by which he would one day make himself the food of others.

Jesus takes the bread and fish, the small contribution that human beings have made. He raises his eyes to heaven, offers the gift to his Father, and says the blessing usually pronounced at meals by the head of a household. This "household," which the apostles had asked to divide into groups of fifty, sits waiting—some chatting, others watching. Jesus continues. He breaks the bread and fish and passes the pieces to the apostles to distribute to the *anawim*, the poor ones of Israel.

At what point the miracle took place, the evangelist does not say. Probably neither he nor the apostles themselves knew exactly when the bread multiplied in the baskets the Twelve were carrying. But, in any case, the food did not run out:

"Blessed are you who are now hungry, for you will be satisfied (Lk 6:21).

The early Christians must have loved retelling the story of that miraculous feeding, for it showed them the Lord's power. It helped them recognize that he who could multiply bread could also multiply his *presence* under the appearance of bread. This miraculous feeding pointed forward to the Eucharist and symbolized it. And the Eucharist itself, of course, looks toward and represents the sacrifice of the cross. It also reminds us that we, too, are called to be "bread broken for many."

Oratio

Lord Jesus, I adore you in this sacrament, which reminds me of all you have done and continue to do for us. You enter our human community in a special way every day during the Eucharistic celebration and remain present in our churches, whether people in the surrounding neighborhoods are aware of this or not. You come to each of us who wishes to receive you, no matter how unworthy and distracted we may be. Help us to see the connection between the Eucharist and our daily lives. Teach us how to be bread broken for the good of our sisters and brothers.

Contemplatio

Bread broken for others.

Solemnities and Feasts
of the Lord and the Saints

Sacred Heart of Jesus—
Year A

⁘ · · · · · · · · · · · ·⁘

Lectio

Matthew 11:25–30

Meditatio

> *" . . . you have revealed them to the childlike."*

Jesus rejoices in the Father, even as he has just rebuked the unrepentant towns for their unbelief. Jesus invites us into his prayer, one full of praise and great joy. The Father and the Son share divine wisdom only with the humble, those who are open to Jesus' words and not blocked by arrogance or prejudice.

Then Jesus extends his great invitation to all who labor and are burdened, that is, to all who live in the valley of tears that is our earthly existence: "Come to me, all you who labor and are burdened, and I will give you rest." I think about what those words meant to the people in the crowd and of what they mean to me. They give meaning to my life and the struggles of my existence. They promise me that the labor will end some day, that a time of rest will come, rest in the Lord's presence and freedom from the heartaches and worries of everyday life.

Jesus assures us that he will help us carry our burdens and show us the way of wisdom. The Feast of the Sacred Heart continues that invitation even to today. It reminds us each year of Jesus' waiting, inviting love for us all. The image of the Sacred Heart of Jesus has found its way into countless homes, factories, offices, schools, beauty parlors, corner stores, gas stations—to the four corners of the earth. That picture of his eternal love for all people is like a golden chain that links all people together under the gentle yoke of the Savior.

May the kingdom of our gentle Lord come, a kingdom of love and joy, a kingdom of the humble and loyal persons to whom Jesus has revealed the Father!

Oratio

Jesus, your heart is a safe refuge for all who carry burdens of pain, betrayal, and disillusionment. I ask you for great trust in your love for me. You showed us the ideal, as, from the cross, you forgave us all with divine compassion. Guide me every day, Jesus, as I walk with you toward the kingdom.

Contemplatio

"Come to me."

Sacred Heart of Jesus— Year B

∴ ⋯⋯⋯⋯⋯ ∴

Lectio

John 19:31–37

Meditatio

> *". . . and immediately blood and water flowed out."*

In today's Gospel the soldiers verify whether Jesus has died. This might seem like an unlikely passage for the Feast of the Sacred Heart when we recall God's immense love and mercy shown to us through his Son. But didn't Jesus himself say, "No one has greater love than this, to lay down one's life for one's friends" (Jn 15:13)? He considers us his friends and worthy enough to die for.

We may wonder why one of the soldiers took his lance and thrust it into Jesus' side, since the text says that they saw he was already dead. The thrust of the spear verifies Jesus' death, and it also shows that Jesus gave himself to the last drop of blood. As the Book of Revelation notes, ". . . every eye will see him, even those who pierced him" (1:7). We see this piercing, and the water and wine that flowed forth, reflected in the mingling of water with blood that occurs daily at the Eucharistic celebrations on all the altars of the world. In the Mass, Christ's sacrifice is renewed, and his love for us is relived.

In Scripture, the concept of heart refers not to the physical organ or the seat of emotions, but rather to the core of the person, the center of each individual. Devotion to the Sacred Heart, then, is honor and adoration of the Person of Jesus Christ. Although symbolized in paintings by Jesus pointing to his heart or holding it in his hand, this devotion consists in knowing and loving the *whole* Christ in his life, teachings, suffering, death, and resurrection.

This devotion was popularized in the Church in the eighteenth century, after the visions of Saint Margaret Mary Alacoque, a French Visitation nun. It seeks to encourage all Christians to deepen the conviction that Jesus loves them immensely.

Jesus Christ, the pierced One who suffered and died for love, never tires of searching for us, forgiving us, and loving us. He wants us to respond by loving him in return, and by living a life according to his Gospel.

Oratio

Sacred Heart of Jesus, your love for each of us is personal and perpetual, lasting throughout all time. It is an awesome gift that you, Lord, God of the universe, want to be loved by us. Do not let us walk away from your love. Increase our trust in you, Heart of Jesus. Amen.

Contemplatio

I will keep my eyes fixed on you, Pierced One!

Sacred Heart of Jesus—
Year C

∴············∴

Lectio

Luke 15:3–7

Meditatio

"What man among you . . . would not leave the ninety-nine?"

In today's Gospel the Pharisees and scribes grumble over the presence of tax collectors and sinners in the crowd listening to Jesus.

In response Jesus asks: If any of you had a flock of sheep, wouldn't you leave the majority to search for a stray that might be in danger?

It's an intriguing question, because for the shepherd to leave his flock *in the wilderness* (perhaps tended only by a couple of dogs) is to place the ninety-nine at risk. Jesus asks them, "Wouldn't you do this?" Perhaps some of his listeners wouldn't. But God is different.

Jesus would soon show the incredible lengths God goes to in rescuing sinners, as we see in Jesus' passion and death. Knowing how much God has done for us in Jesus, we realize that the Lord won't give up on anyone as long as that person has breath. God keeps giving each of us another chance.

If we don't think we need that new chance, let's ask for the grace to know ourselves better. Original sin has left all of us self-centered and grasping. May we recognize our need to throw ourselves into the arms of God's mercy with true sorrow and the determination to really change!

When we better understand our own need for forgiveness and more clearly see the breadth and depth of God's mercy, our compassion should be stirred for one another and for the poor unfortunates who are victimized by the evils of our society. Let's never give up on any strays we know personally. Saint Monica didn't give up on her son Augustine—and look at the results!

Oratio

Lord Jesus, Master and Shepherd, I thank you for your loving Heart, which spurred you on to give your life for me. Help me shake off my complacency and see myself as the sinner that I am. Support me, lest in recognizing my sinfulness I become paralyzed—too disheartened to move on. Teach me true sorrow. Show me the steps I must take to become less self-centered and more like you. Guide me along the right path. I want to pray also for persons I know or have heard about who need your help. Rescue all of us from selfishness and sin, and bring us safely home to the welcoming embrace of your Father. Amen.

Contemplatio

"Lord, may I know myself; may I know you" (Saint Augustine).

Presentation of the Lord
February 2

⁘ · · · · · · · · · · · ⁘

Lectio

   Luke 2:22–40

Meditatio

> *". . . a light for revelation to the Gentiles*
> *and glory for your people Israel."*

Enlightened by the inspiration of the Holy Spirit, Simeon has come to the temple in Jerusalem. The Holy Spirit promised him that he would not die before seeing "the Christ of the Lord." By inspiration, he approaches a young mother, Mary, and her husband, Joseph. They are bringing her first-born son, Jesus, who is only forty days old, to offer him to the Lord God as the Law of Moses requires. Simeon's face is aglow, his eyes bright with great joy as he reaches out to take the child in his own arms. He is overwhelmed with happiness as he gazes on the tiny face looking up at him. At last! This is he, the Christ he has waited so long to see! Now he thanks God who has, in this small child, sent "a light for revelation to the Gentiles" and glory for Israel. God himself has come to his Temple to meet his people. But the light of revelation is given for the Gentiles as well. Light has entered the world, shattering the darkness. All people are to see salvation from their sins. Simeon can die now; he has waited long to see this day, and God has kept his promise.

How does this beautiful story in the Gospel impact my life today? Perhaps, like Simeon, I have experienced recently the fulfillment of God's promise. Or perhaps I am still waiting to see how God is at work in some difficult area of my life. The long wait for the coming of the Savior did not extinguish Simeon's faith. But it can be hard to keep one's faith burning brightly in the absence of a clear sign of God's power and presence. The word of God, the sacraments of Eucharist and Reconciliation, and daily prayer help us in our longing and waiting for the grace of God.

Oratio

Lord Jesus, I come to you to receive your light of faith, a deeper faith, and to find you in the "temple" of my life. I do desire a deeper relationship with you, and I seek you in the sacraments and in praying with the word. You know what I am waiting and longing for. Increase my faith. Send your Holy Spirit upon me as you sent him upon Simeon. Help me to reveal you and your goodness to others, to let your light shine through me. Amen.

Contemplatio

Come Holy Spirit, enlighten me now, in this present moment.

Saint Joseph, Husband of Mary
March 19

❖ · · · · · · · · · · · · ❖

Lectio

Luke 2:41–51

Meditatio

> " . . . *his mother said to him* . . ."

Where is Joseph? As I prayed with this passage, his absence from this Gospel reading on his feast day overwhelmed me. Or was it his silence?

Jewish fathers were required to introduce their sons to the Law. Perhaps Jesus' parents were getting him accustomed to keeping the Law by bringing him with them to the Passover feast in Jerusalem. Going home, it takes a day before Mary and Joseph realize he is not with them, for men and women traveled in separate groups. They return to Jerusalem and for three days search for Jesus. The Greek word signifies a thorough, prolonged search. They scour Jerusalem, looking up and down every street, without rest.

Finally, they find Jesus in the Temple, quietly asking questions to the teachers of the Law. Mary speaks: "Why have you done this to us?" But Joseph speaks no word and shows no expression of irritation or anger. He is conspicuous by the veil that hides him from our eyes.

As a father, a laborer, a provider for the family, he has every right to be upset. He has lost days of work, not to mention the toll that anxiety and sleepless nights have taken on him. And it isn't as if Jesus had been kidnapped or was searching for them. No, he isn't even concerned about his family, but is off talking to the teachers. Now Joseph has to travel back to Nazareth with Mary and Jesus on unsafe roads, without the protection of the larger group of pilgrims. Many a man's blood would be boiling. But Joseph keeps silent.

After reading this Gospel, I read the account of the woman caught in adultery. She is thrust in front of Jesus by angry teachers of the Law. "What should be done with her?" they demand. He diverts their angry eyes from her by drawing in the sand, not wanting to get involved in their raging schemes. At last he tells the one without sin to cast the first stone. Then he returns to his doodling in the sand. Where did he learn that strategy? Was it from Joseph? I like that man.

Oratio

Joseph, I long for your silence, for your wonder, for your respect for what is, for your trust that the Father has your life in his hands—always. Help me.

Contemplatio

Rest. Wait. Trust. Rest.

Annunciation
March 25

❖ ⋯⋯⋯⋯⋯ ❖

Luke 1:26–38

"Behold, I am the handmaid of the Lord.
May it be done to me according to your word."

Two themes emerge as I pray over the Scripture passage for the Feast of the Annunciation: the mystery of *God's will*, and the response of *faith*. In Jesus and Mary, these come together in harmony.

When the Angel Gabriel greets Mary as "full of grace," she is troubled. "Do not be afraid, Mary," the angel reassures her. Fear, our natural human response, is silenced only in the face of faith. To echo the words of another Gospel passage, "Do not be afraid; just have faith" (Mk 5:36). Mary says with faith, "May it be done to me according to your word." In other words, may your will be done.

Mary's assent expresses her profound trust in God, without seeing where her yes will lead. Mary is open to the gift of a new life within her, the life of God himself within her womb. Willing to risk the consequences of what this might mean for her, she opens herself totally to the plan of God. Only faith and love could make this possible. But for God, whom Mary was united to in her whole self, nothing is impossible.

The Letter to the Hebrews from today's first reading, referring to Christ, parallels Mary's words in today's Gospel when it quotes Psalm 40:7–8: "Behold, I come to do your will." In obedience to the plan of the Father, Christ takes on human flesh. "And the Word became flesh and made his dwelling among us" (Jn 1:14). The Son of God loved us so much, he became one of us!

The mystery of God's will and Christ becoming flesh call me, call us, to gratitude, as well as to attentiveness to the annunciations God whispers or speaks in our lives. As it happened for Mary, Christ can take on flesh in us in the measure in which we open our lives in faith to follow God's plan for us. Christ can grow imperceptibly until one day, we can say with Saint Paul, "yet I live, no longer I, but Christ lives in me" (Gal 2:20).

Oratio

I praise and thank you, Lord, for becoming human like us, in order to make us like you. Increase my faith daily. May my trust flow from a greater awareness of your goodness, mercy, and love. As I grow in trust, may I grow in a desire to follow your loving will for me in all things. I want to cooperate in your plan for my life. Mary, pray for us now and always.

Contemplatio

Yes, Lord. May your will be done in my life.

Birth of John the Baptist
June 24

⁑· · · · · · · · · · · ·⁑

Lectio

Luke 1:57–66, 80

Meditatio

"He will be called John."

"There is no one among your relatives who has this name." This is a humorous scene—the mother proclaiming her son's name and the well-wishers protesting that there must have been a mistake! And then the guests (forgetting that the child's father isn't deaf, but only speechless) *ask him by signs* what the child is to be called!

The vignette becomes more serious when Zechariah writes: "John is his name," and the guests realize that divine intervention is still at work in the lives of this elderly couple.

Both Jesus and John received their names through intermediaries *from God himself.* Jesus was named "God saves." John was named "gift."

In Israel's past, God had changed Abram's name to Abraham, Sarai's to Sarah and Jacob's to Israel. This suggests that names are important to God. Some people think that God has given each of us a special name also (see Rv 2:17). It's an intriguing thought. Would our personal "God-name" reflect something we do or something we are? Would it reflect our unique relationship with the tender Father who called us into being? Would it mirror one of his attributes? Certainly, it would somehow denote our unrepeatable individuality.

Perhaps all our identities—although each of them is unique—are related to that simple, common name "John." Karol Wojtyla, as a contributor to the Vatican II documents and later as John Paul II, wrote more than once that none of us human beings can find ourselves except by making a *gift* of self. When we reflect on what is known about the Trinity, it fits. The circulation of life among the three divine Persons is *giving*. The activity of the Trinity in the universe is *giving*. We humans are made in the image and likeness of God, so. . . .

What does this mean for me? How am I to be "gift"?

Oratio

Jesus, you are a gift to us. You were the Father's gift to us as an infant; you gave your life for us as an adult; and you continue to give yourself to us in the word, as well as in the Eucharist and the other sacraments. Help me to understand the ways I can be a gift to you and to others. To whom in particular do you wish me to be a gift?

You may want to spend more time later today, in a quiet place, praying for insights about how God is calling you to give of yourself.

Contemplatio

I have received freely; I want to give freely (see Mt 10:8).

Saints Peter and Paul, Apostles
June 29

⁘ · · · · · · · · · · · · ⁘

Lectio

Matthew 16:13–19

Meditatio

> *"For flesh and blood has not revealed this to you."*

Simon Peter stands as still as the huge building block whose name he bears. He is suddenly oblivious to his surroundings—the lush vegetation and fragrant flowers of the district of Caesarea Philippi.

Jesus is looking at him intently, and without shifting his gaze, Peter knows that the other apostles, too, are staring at him. He has always been their spokesman.

Jesus repeats his question: "But who do *you* say that I am?"

Just before Jesus asked, the rugged fisherman had realized where the conversation was going. In a flash of illumination he understood what the response should be. But he can't find the words to articulate his newfound knowledge. "You are the Messiah . . ." he begins tentatively. But that isn't enough; he knows he has to say more. Suddenly the words come to him clearly and he blurts out: "the Son of the living God!"

Peter's declaration *must* have been made somewhat like this, because, as Jesus pointed out, the fisherman couldn't have come up with the answer himself or learned it from human beings. The Father in heaven enlightened him. For both Peter and Paul (see Gal 1:16), it was the Father who revealed the identity of the Son.

These two pillars of the Church we commemorate today were outwardly very different men, each with strengths and weaknesses, both intensely devoted to Jesus. And the Lord was devoted to them, too. He sustained them to the end of their earthly lives and received them into his kingdom, to live with him forever.

The Church established by Jesus on the foundation of the apostles has always been humanly weak, as Peter and Paul were. Yet it has survived threats from without and schisms from within, enduring for 2,000 years while nations and empires have fallen on all sides. The presence and power of the Lord keep it firm and steadfast.

Oratio

Lord God, like Peter, Paul, and the Church itself, I'm weak and unsure. But the example of the apostles and the Church show me that you enlighten and sustain the weak. Paul wrote that when he was weak, he was made strong by the power of your grace. Keep me from giving up; sustain me as you did the apostles. Help me to follow the example of your saints.

Contemplatio

"Power is made perfect in weakness" (2 Cor 12:9).

List of Contributors

∴· · · · · · · · · · · ·∵

Celebrate the Church's great seasons of grace by praying
lectio divina with the Daughters of St. Paul.

ADVENT GRACE
Daily Gospel Reflections
By the Daughters of St. Paul
0-8198-0787-7
$7.95

LENTEN GRACE
Daily Gospel Reflections
By the Daughters of St. Paul
0-8198-4525-6
$7.95

Continue to celebrate the grace of God in everyday life
through *lectio divina* with the Daughters of St. Paul.

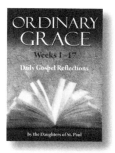

ORDINARY GRACE
Weeks 1–17
Daily Gospel Reflections
By the Daughters of St. Paul
0-8198-5442-5
$9.95

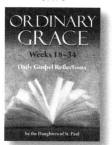

ORDINARY GRACE
Weeks 18–34
Daily Gospel Reflections
By the Daughters of St. Paul
0-8198-5443-3
$9.95

Order at www.pauline.org, or by calling Pauline Books & Media at
1-800-876-4463, or through the book and media center nearest you.

BOOKS & MEDIA

The Daughters of St. Paul operate book and media centers at the following addresses. Visit, call or write the one nearest you today, or find us on the World Wide Web, www.pauline.org

CALIFORNIA
3908 Sepulveda Blvd, Culver City, CA 90230   310-397-8676
935 Brewster Avenue, Redwood City, CA 94063   650-369-4230
5945 Balboa Avenue, San Diego, CA 92111   858-565-9181
FLORIDA
145 S.W. 107th Avenue, Miami, FL 33174   305-559-6715
HAWAII
1143 Bishop Street, Honolulu,HI 96813   808-521-2731
Neighbor Islands call: 866-521-2731
ILLINOIS
172 North Michigan Avenue, Chicago, IL 60601   312-346-4228
LOUISIANA
4403 Veterans Memorial Blvd, Metairie, LA 70006   504-887-7631
MASSACHUSETTS
885 Providence Hwy, Dedham, MA 02026   781-326-5385
MISSOURI
9804 Watson Road, St. Louis, MO 63126   314-965-3512
NEW YORK
150 East 52nd Street, New York, NY 10022   212-754-1110
PENNSYLVANIA
Philadelphia—relocating   215-969-5068
SOUTH CAROLINA
243 King Street, Charleston,SC 29401   843-577-0175
VIRGINIA
1025 King Street, Alexandria, VA 22314   703-549-3806
CANADA
3022 Dufferin Street, Toronto, ON M6B 3T5   416-781-9131

¡También somos su fuente para libros, videos
y música en español!